Fred Cusick

VOICE OF THE BRUINS

Fred Cusick

SP

SPORTS
PUBLISHING
L.L.C.

SportsPublishingLLC.com

ISBN-10: 1-58261-981-6
ISBN-13: 978-1-58261-981-1

All interior photographs are courtesy of Fred Cusick unless otherwise noted.

Publishers: Peter L. Bannon and Joseph J. Bannon Sr.
Senior managing editor: Susan M. Moyer
Acquisitions editor: Mike Pearson
Developmental editor: Doug Hoepker and Suzanne Perkins
Art director: K. Jeffrey Higgerson
Dust jacket design: JosephT. Brumleve
Interior layout: Joseph T. Brumleve and Kathryn R. Holleman
Photo editor: Erin Linden-Levy

Sports Publishing L.L.C.
804 North Neil Street
Champaign, IL 61820
Phone: 1-877-424-2665
Fax: 217-363-2073
www.SportsPublishingLLC.com

Printed in the United States of America

Library of Congress Cataloging-in-Publication Data

Cusick, Fred, 1918-
    Fred Cusick : voice of the Bruins / Fred Cusick.
      p. cm.
    ISBN-13: 978-1-58261-981-1 (soft cover : alk. paper)
    ISBN-10: 1-58261-981-6 (soft cover : alk. paper)
    1. Cusick, Fred, 1918- 2. Sportscasters--United States--Biography. 3. Boston Bruins (Hockey team) I. Title.
GV742.42.C87A3 2007
070.4'49796092--dc22
[B]
                              2006029597

To my wife, Barbara

Contents

Acknowledgments

This book started as notes to my grandchildren—Julia, Marie, and Katharine—to share with them some of the stories of my life.

While writing this book, I had the encouragement and support of my daughters—Martha, Sarah, and Mary—and my son and daughter-in-law—Ted and Laurie. The Mullins have also provided tremendous assistance: Ann, Kate, Hugh, Kim, and Walter.

CHAPTER ONE

The Best Seat in the House

For over 40 years, my "office" was an overhang off the first balcony on the south side of the Boston Garden. While I am probably best known for my connection to the Boston Bruins— announcing their games on radio and TV for 44 years—it's really the Garden that was my second home.

From my perch I called over 1,500 games (plus 1,500 more on the road), surrounded by the noise of the cheering of sellout crowds. Originally, when I was named the Bruins announcer in 1952, I called the game from a plywood enclosure above the press area at the Boston Garden. The booth dampened a lot of the crowd noise that was so much a part of the game.

But after I moved to the overhang, thunderous noise echoed across the arena as I sat with an open microphone to describe the exciting action below. No extra "crowd mike" was needed to relay the roar from the fans as Bobby Orr made one of his incomparable rushes, Terry O'Reilly dealt one of his jolting body checks, and Phil

Esposito scored deftly on a rebound. Who can forget the bumper sticker that many fans had on their cars: "Jesus saves and Esposito scores on the rebound." Fans (all 13,909 of them) didn't just attend a hockey game—they participated in it. No organ riffs, recorded trumpet blasts, or exhortations to "cheer" were needed to stimulate the sell-out crowd. From the best seat in the house, I had a clear and unimpeded view of the players. No helmets or face masks were worn, so there was no need to search for their numbers to identify them.

Like Fenway Park's famous Green Monster, the Boston Garden was part of the game. Built in 1929, the large tan edifice was a replica of Madison Square Garden in New York. "Garden" would seem an unlikely name to give to a building erected to house hockey and boxing.

I always felt that the most intimidating factor for opponents was the size and structure of the Garden. The rink was 191 feet long and 83 feet wide. A standard rink was 200 by 85. The angle of the seats seemingly had the fans looming over the ice and cheering loudly for their home team. The roar of the people created claustrophobic thoughts in the visitors' mind, and probably was worth a goal a game for the Bruins. There was no message board—just a serviceable scoreboard that displayed the game clock, the score, penalized players' numbers, and shots on net.

When Don Cherry was the Bruins' coach during their powerhouse years in the 1970s, he put together an aggressive team that seemed to enjoy throwing a hard-hitting check on an opponent in the tight enclosure more than they enjoyed scoring a goal. Many a rival player plainly indicated his dislike of the place.

When I called the games, luxury boxes didn't exist. If someone in business wanted to entertain a client, it was more than likely a quick bite at Polcari's restaurant in the Italian North End before the start of the game. At the old Garden, people came to watch hockey.

The Gallery Gods

Unique to the Garden was a collection of die-hard and voluble fans known as the Gallery Gods. The Gallery Gods were an organized group, seated near the rafters, who monitored their own behavior for attendance and actions. They knew the game well—as did nearly all the Bruins fans. In my mind, no other team in the league had a group comparable to them. And they didn't just save their comments for the opposing team.

In a rare quiet moment, a vociferous Gallery God would yell a pithy comment praising or faulting a Bruin or opponent. In 1966, Harry Sinden had a rocky start as a first-year Bruins coach after having achieved great success in Oklahoma City. Winning only 17 games out of 70, the Bruins finished last. During one losing game, a loud comment from the Gallery was: "Hey Harry, there's a bus leaving for Oklahoma in the morning. Be there—under it."

Another time, the genial King Clancy, a Hall of Fame defenseman from Toronto who loved to banter with the Boston fans, heard a yell from the Gallery: "Hey Clancy, we got a town named for you," (a pause as Clancy looked up) "MARBLEHEAD!" Clancy just laughed. Orland Kurtenbach, a journeyman center, told a Boston sports writer that he was off to a slow start because he didn't really get going until Christmastime. Some of the Gallery Gods showed up at the opening game of the season in October with Santa Claus outfits, and all joined in a chorus of "Jingle Bells." There was even advice for Bobby Orr, on his way to Rookie-of-the-Year honors, while the club was headed for the cellar. From the upper reaches of the Garden came the cry: "Hey Bobby, slow down, you're making the team look bad."

Memorable Days

In 1970, from my "best seat" location, I described the Stanley Cup-winning goal by Bobby Orr in the overtime victory over St. Louis on WBZ radio. Its clear channel signal was heard in 38 states, and you can be sure that from whatever area they were listening, most of the audience on that hot May day was rooting for Bobby and the Bruins. I treasure the tape I have of the play-by-play of the action, including the winning goal.

I called hockey games at the Garden for 43 of its 67 years of existence. On Saturday afternoons in 1948, I broadcast the Greater Boston Interscholastic Hockey League games on WVOM—a small Brookline, Massachusetts, radio station. Four games meant absorbing the lineups of eight high school teams—a total of 120 players. It was great training.

In 1950–1951, I covered the Boston Olympics—a team of local players who had been stars while playing high school or college hockey in the Boston area. In 1936, Walter Brown, the general manager of the Boston Garden, had been the manager of the United States Olympic Hockey Team. Most of the players were from the Greater Boston area. Walter simply adopted the name "Olympics" and had the team play at the Boston Garden. They were an instant hit. The roster soon became filled with local players. Tom Moon (Lexington), Paul Guibord (Melrose), Eddie Barry (Wellesley), and Cliff Thompson (Stoneham), were representative of the team's local flavor. At their peak they would draw 16,000 fans to the Garden on

Sunday afternoons. In the evenings, the Bruins would draw another 16,000–32,000 fans in one day was proof positive that New England was hockey country.

Another tradition of the Garden is the annual Beanpot Tournament—usually a scrappy matchup among local college teams: Boston University, Boston College, Harvard, and Northeastern (my alma mater). One year I did the play-by-play of the games—not an easy assignment. Hockey analyst Bob Norton helped me, and I was most impressed with his work, so much so I later wrote him a letter of appreciation. Identifying about 70 players was a difficult task, and I was glad Bob was there.

Whether high school, college, or professional hockey was the venue, the Boston Garden provided the intimate atmosphere that added intensity to the competition. The acoustic system (or lack of one) magnified the cheering and made attendance at the game a night to remember. The last hurrah for the Garden, its players, and fans was September 29, 1995. For me, the occasion was sad. I lost the best seat in the house.

Location, Location, Location—Other Rinks

As in real estate, it is *location, location, location* for sportscasters. I was fortunate with my "best seat" in the Boston Garden but not so lucky in other arenas. One of my toughest assignments was broadcasting the 1988 Boston/New Jersey Devils Playoff series.

The Bruins were on the verge of making it to the finals in Stanley Cup competition. After splitting two home games against New Jersey, they played game three at the Brendan Byrne Arena. Throughout the

Arena's history, our broadcast location had been mid-ice, adjacent to the main cameras, and overhanging the first balcony. It was an excellent spot, comparable to Boston Garden—the best in the League. To my consternation, I discovered that because ESPN was televising, the new location would be an improvised one behind the last row of seats in the Arena. It was by far the worst seat in the house. Instead of appropriating four seats next to the ESPN setup, a hastily built platform, shaky desk, and monitor were situated almost touching the rafters. I protested vigorously to Dan Berkery, the general manager of TV 38, who was at the game. He tried to calm me down by suggesting that a new and satisfactory position would be found for the next game at the Byrne Arena. Calling the game was an ordeal, but a 6–1 victory by Boston made the horrendous location palatable.

Following the game, Jim Schoenfeld, the Devils coach, exploded at referee Don Koharski as he was leaving the ice. "Have another doughnut, you fat pig," was clearly heard, and there were reports of a shoving match with Koharski—either slipping or stumbling from some kind of contact. The "pig" reference reverberated around the league because virtually everybody knew that the location of the Meadowland complex, including the arena, was once a gigantic pig farm. The next day, Schoenfeld was suspended by the National Hockey League, but the Devils went to the New Jersey Supreme Court and got a restraining order that allowed Schoenfeld to coach in game four. When he took his position behind the bench ready to start the game, the NHL officials assigned left the ice and would not officiate. After almost an hour's delay, three amateur hockey officials who were part-time employees of the Devils, took on the job. All this off-stage maneuvering was not relayed to our visiting broadcast platform high in the rafters of Brendan Byrne Arena. There was no change in our horrific position. We had to guess what was going on. The million or so viewing fans would not be interested in an explanation of a poor position. They would assume that our New Jersey location would be just like the one at Boston Garden. The game went on, and I never did hear any complaints about the call. The Bruins lost the game 3–1, but went on to win the series in seven games.

Game six found me sitting in the same terrible area, where I had to call the game over the heads of the last-row patrons who were raucous and noisy in their support of the home team. It was a series where the National Hockey League reached below the level of the World Wrestling Federation and somehow survived. The visiting play-by-play television and radio broadcaster is at the mercy of the home team in regard to where he is located.

There is no standard for broadcasting locations in the National Hockey League. The sportscasters have an organization (they pick the Coach of the Year), but they have no voice in selecting a site to broadcast. As of my retirement in 1998, Pittsburgh had the worst. Oddly enough, the best was the new United Air Lines Arena in Chicago. Chicago ownership was ambivalent about television. They thought that televised home games would diminish their sellout crowds, so they never did it. Yet in the new building they placed the key cameras and the location of the visiting broadcasters in the first balcony, with ample room for interviews. It was easily the best seat in the house. It should be the model for the League.

CHAPTER TWO

Bobby Orr: The Greatest Player of All

Gordie Howe was powerful, and he created space for himself by the sheer force of his play. Wayne Gretzky was like a bird, weaving and floating through the air. Rocket Richard was dynamic and unstoppable from the opposition's blue line in. Jean Belliveau was a flawless talent—tall and steady—and he usually dominated a game while he was on the ice. Mario Lemieux makes No. 2. He was truly a great talent.

But without a doubt, the best hockey player of the 20th century was Bobby Orr. He is a legend—and, in my opinion, he deserves to be. *The Boston Globe* conducted a poll in the 1970s asking who the greatest athlete in Boston's history was. Bobby was the winner— beating Ted Williams, Bill Russell, Carl Yastrzemski, and Bob Cousy. He controlled the game with his ability to set the pace.

His play took me back to the days when I was just learning the game on Chandler's Pond in Brighton. On occasion, the Boston College hockey team practiced there, even though there was no rink set up. After their practice, some of the BC players would join in our scrimmage, and when that ended, they would hang around. I remember one player, Peter Murphy, who would take part in a game of keep away. He would simply retain possession of the puck with great stickhandling and deking (in hockey, that means making a deceptive move that lures a player out of position). We were high school players, and we could not stop him. Bobby Orr could do that in a confined area. He thrived on killing penalties and, once in a while, would top off his dazzling display with a shorthanded goal.

The Discovery of Bobby Orr

If Ganonoque, Ontario, was the Bruins' Bethlehem, then one of the wise men was certainly a scout named Wren Blair. In the Bruins' franchise history, Wren Blair should rank high on the list of contributors. He was a true hockey man, whose record includes providing his expertise to many amateur and professional franchises. During his career, Wren was a scout, manager, owner, coach, and entrepreneur for a variety of teams, ranging from the Clinton Comets of the Eastern League, to the Minnesota North Stars of the National Hockey League. He zoomed into the headlines across Canada in 1958, when he led the Whitby Dunlops to a World Championship by defeating the Russians in Oslo, Norway. Harry Sinden, a future coach and general manager of the Bruins, was one of his star players.

Later, while managing the Kingston Frontenacs (a farm team of the Bruins), Wren Blair joined four other members of the Bruins organization at Ganonoque to scout a couple of players named Eaton and Higgins. At the game—featuring 14- and 15-year-old players— Bruins owner Weston Adams, chief scout Baldy Cotton, general manager Lynn Patrick and coach Milt Schmidt, along with Blair focused their attention on a 12-year-old who played the entire game on defense and was easily the most talented player on the ice. He was Bobby Orr.

But Bobby Orr could not be signed to a Junior A contract until he was 14. Everyone at the rink that day agreed he would be worth pursuing. The assignment went to Wren Blair to keep in touch with the Orr family living in Parry Sound. It was a two-year effort.

In the history book *Boston Bruins: Celebrating 75 Years,* published by Tehabi Books, Harry Sinden is quoted: "Wren is the guy who hung around Parry Sound for months, talked with the parents constantly...Wren was the guy who persevered."

Blair's first move was to secure sponsorship of the Parry Sound Minor Hockey Association by the Bruins. He arranged for Milt Schmidt to come to the packed meeting at the Town Hall to hear the Bruins' presentation. Milt had a well-known name throughout Canada for his brilliant play with the Bruins and his Hall of Fame membership. The town gladly accepted the sponsorship and the $1,000 that went with it.

Bobby Orr turned 14 in March 1962. Would the two-year effort of Wren Blair pay off? In his book, *The Bird,* published by Quarry Press Inc., Blair points out that Weston Adams personally visited the Orrs and tried to get the young man's and his father's signature on a Junior A card. When he failed, he called Blair and turned the assignment over to him. Adams must have been crushed by the rejection.

Over a Labor Day weekend, Blair visited the Orr family a couple of times, and dutifully reported to Adams his failure to get the signatures. Blair continued to meet with the Orr family and finally prevailed. Bobby and his father signed the card of the Oshawa Generals—a Bruins-sponsored Junior A team. This contract bound him to Boston for his NHL career.

Getting that 14-year-old's signature wasn't easy. Every team knew of his talent. His coach in Parry Sound was Bucko Macdonald, a former Detroit Red Wing, who assured Blair at Ganonoque that Orr was in line to sign with Detroit. Another concern was Orr's mother. She was reluctant to see her teenager leave home permanently and attend a distant school. The Bruins and Blair fortunately had a solution. The Oshawa rink was being rebuilt. It wasn't ready, so the Generals would play their home games at Maple Leaf Gardens. Bobby Orr would live at home and commute—even though the Maple Leaf Gardens was 100 miles away. Most of the games were played on weekends, and the occasional weekday game would not be a burden. Mrs. Orr came on board.

Made for TV

Talk about timing. The Bruins had finished out of the playoffs for seven straight years when the teenager who was to be their savior appeared. Also arriving on the Boston scene were two independent television stations with deep-pocket owners looking for sports programming. Channel 38 had been around for a couple of years, but under the ownership of the Archdiocese of Boston, it did not have much money for programming or rights fees. In 1966, it was purchased by Storer Broadcasting, owner of many network stations. Channel 56 was to be launched by Christmastime of 1966. It was owned by Kaiser Industries, and the company planned to install independent stations around the country. Kaiser signed the Celtics to a three-year contract, but the Bruins were signed for only one. Both team managements were leery about having home games televised, so it was road games only.

When Orr arrived in Boston at the age of 18, he was able to distinguish himself, and, save for a far-fetched idea advanced by General Manager Hap Emms, he gave every indication of being the star he was to become. At a game in Detroit, Emms suggested to coach Harry Sinden that Orr, who had always played defense—a position that allowed him to control a game, to set its pace, to create the space for launching spectacular rushes—be moved to center. He was playing against the vaunted Red Wings: Howe, Lindsay, and Abel up front, and Kelley and Pronovost on defense—an impregnable group. How formidable? To begin with, they didn't allow you to have the puck too often. Most of the play was in the Bruins' end. When Bobby tried to move up the middle, he was sandwiched by the potent Detroit defense. It was a dreadful experiment and short lived.

Channel 56 was unimpressed with the Bruins' ratings. They refused to match a more lucrative bid that came from Channel 38 for the next season's broadcast rights. It was a terrible mistake. Channel 56 was operating from a tower in Woburn, Massachusetts, that was simply not high enough to cover Greater Boston. If you lived in South Boston, you could only get a blurred signal. People didn't watch the station, so how could management expect the Orr-led Bruins to get any kind of a rating?

The blond, youthful, good-looking young man attracted even non-fans to the telecasts on Channel 38. Never has one man had such an impact on a sport, and those affiliated with it, as Orr did with the Bruins. Every game became a sellout that brought added revenue to the team. Channel 38 became a force on the Boston television scene.

From 1969 through 1972, the rating for regular-season games (regardless of the opposition) was 25. That meant one in four of Boston TV homes would be watching—about a million people. All New England was clamoring to see Bobby Orr, so Channel 38 was the beneficiary of expanded cable coverage. When Orr was on TV38, it would cause a 25-percent decline in viewers of the three network affiliates, who had the market all to themselves before the arrival of Channels 38 and 56. Orr also had a huge impact on the number of skating rinks built for hockey and public skating. At the height of the interest, there were 52 private rinks in operation and 44 operated by the state.

I joined Channel 38 as play-by-play announcer in 1971, and I covered just about every regular-season and playoff game for the rest of Orr's career. He was a joy to watch. His mother, Marva, rarely went to see him play, but she was in attendance once at a game in Toronto. Bobby scored three goals. It had to be a tribute to her. With his superb shot and all-around skills he could score, but his usual pattern was to make the big rush and set up somebody else. And then, having clearly been the star of the game, he would hide out in the trainer's room so that others could take bows for what was usually a winning effort by the team.

Various coaches thought they could devise means to stop Orr, or at least control him. If they sent two men after Bobby, Orr would just as quickly pass off to the open Bruin, and another attack would be launched. Scotty Bowman, coach of the St. Louis Blues, thought he had the solution when he brought his team to the finals in 1970.

The Bruins were looking for their first Stanley Cup in the Orr regime. Bowman thought that he could take Orr out of the game by assigning veteran forward Jim Roberts to shadow him all over the ice.

The idea was to have Roberts stay no more than a yard or two from Orr, no matter where he was on the ice. It didn't matter whether Orr had the puck or not. Orr quickly caught on to the tactic and simply skated to a position, well away from the puck, taking Roberts with him. The Bruins and Blues were then in a five-against-five situation, exactly as we see it now in overtime. The Boston five were more talented than the St. Louis five, and they soon were scoring goals and putting the game out of reach. The experiment didn't last too long. Orr and Roberts returned to their regular assignments.

In hockey, the best fighters seldom fight. They establish their reputations early, and therefore nobody takes them on. Of course, some tough guys made a living out of stirring up trouble. Dave Schultz and Terry O'Reilly were among the leaders in that category. I recall Ed Sandford, a solid Bruins winger, clearly beating up a brash Montreal rookie, Dickie Moore, at the Forum. He did it so decisively that few players challenged him the rest of his career.

The Bobby Orr situation was different. He was the star player who put in a lot of ice time each game. Why didn't rival coaches designate one of their average players to take Orr on and hopefully take him out of the game for a five-minute penalty? They didn't do it, and the main reason was that Orr could fight. He had 39 fights in his nine-year career, and I recall that only Wilf Paiement of Vancouver might have out-pointed him. His natural ability made him a talented fighter, so he seldom had to take on rival battlers.

The Chicago Deal

Unfortunately for Orr, he had as his agent Alan Eagleson, who rarely came to Boston—so I don't think he fully realized the popularity of the young man in New England. Bobby had an almost equal impact in Canada. Eagleson was content to sign up the Orr name to just about any deal imaginable north of the border. While in Toronto, covering the Bruins, I saw a billboard advertising Bobby Orr Pizza. There was no class to the Eagleson direction.

In 1975, Bobby had an accumulation of knee operations, and the Bruins wisely had a physical exam to determine how long a contract should be negotiated. The team's medical examiners said that there were not too many miles left in the damaged knees. That analysis proved to be 100-percent correct. Realizing that keeping Orr affiliated with the Bruins, even though he could not play, was important, the Bruins made Orr an offer. However, Eagleson had him sign a million-dollar deal with the Chicago Blackhawks.

A press conference was called at the Hotel Somerset after Orr signed with Chicago. I was there, and you could cut the gloomy atmosphere with a knife. I recall telling Bill Watters, a well-connected hockey man who was in the Eagleson entourage, that Bobby Orr could spend the rest of his life touring New England, and he would never get to meet all of the New Englanders who wanted to thank him for his exciting play. In the Chicago lineup, Orr was not even an average player—his All-Star luster was gone. In three years with the team, he played in only 26 games. He proved useless to Chicago, and he couldn't wait to get back to New England. I recall a Bruins game in Chicago Stadium, and Bobby Orr was walking through the lobby. Hardly anyone knew him.

Fortunately, Bobby came back to the Boston area after Chicago, and now spends much of his time meeting the fans who have unforgettable memories of his accomplishments. I've had the pleasure of seeing him play in person (probably more than anybody else), and

I believe he is the greatest player of all. While I am not a poet by any means, his amazing talent inspired me to write this tribute to Bobby.

The Ballad of Bobby Orr

It was Christmastime in the sixties
And the Bruins needed a gift
A star of certain stature
To give the team a lift.

In a League of six, their fortunes fell
Each year they finished low.
The fans, though, never left them
Their hopes stayed ever aglow.
The scouts fanned out, 'cross village and town
No stone was left unturned
To find the player or players
In whom talent and stardom burned.

One night in Ganonoque
In search of that talent rare
A group of Bruin leaders
Were led by scout Wren Blair.

A bantam game in progress
Gave promise of prospects in store
But the eyes of all soon focused
On a lad named Bobby Orr.

At the age of twelve, on a team in their teens,
His talent quickly shone
So plans were made to sign him up
Before his rights were gone.

But rules proclaimed: "No signing"
'Til he was fourteen years, at least,
So the Bruins began their planning
And their efforts never ceased.

To Blair went the job of courting
The parents, who showed concern
About how he'd be directed
And facilities for him to learn

They finally conceded, and a form was signed,
And the Bruins sighed with relief,
He played for their team in Oshawa
In a manner beyond belief.

Still in his teens he was ready
To play for the Black and the Gold,
He made his debut 'gainst the Red Wings
One look, and the fans were sold.

He controlled the game from the blue line
With speed and dash and flair
As TV captured his exploits
All New England knew he was rare.

But more was needed on a last-place team
To add to the skill of an Orr,
So Fred and Ken and Espo
Were joined by even more.

And then, in place, they made a run
For the Stanley Cup was their aim,
In 1970, they won it at last
As his goal brought lasting fame.

His career abridged by wounded knees
His star stayed its brightest hue
Despite the pain, he led the team
To a title in '72.

Two Cups secured—could there be more?
Fate quickly intervened
World Hockey interceded
And from the Bruins some talent was weaned.

The heritage of Bobby's deeds
Was international acclaim.
Eight Norris Awards and All-Star play
And Induction to the Hall of Fame

But best of all he's among us
For business, for charities and more,
His family, his golf, his friendship
Add to the Legend of Orr.

He's a gift that keeps on giving
And that is the best by far,
He's ageless we know, as we bask in the glow
Of the Twentieth Century's star.

CHAPTER THREE

Carefree Days

In 1918, Armistice and the great flu epidemic made the headlines. It was also the year I was born.

I grew up during the '20s and '30s in an Irish Catholic enclave in Brighton, a neighborhood on the west side of Boston about six miles as the crow flies from the Boston Garden.

The names of people who either owned or rented on our street testified to their nation of origin: Kane, Doherty, Kennedy, Sullivan, Kiley, Gannon, Lynch, and Reardon were our neighbors. "Cusick" is not an Irish-sounding name, and as I moved about later in my service with the Navy and my broadcasting career, many people thought it was Polish or Czechoslovakian in origin. But I had deep roots in Ireland.

Both my father and mother were born in County Galway; my mother, Bridget Donohue, in a village called Tuam, and my father, Michael Cusick, in Kinvara. Neither of them talked about the transformation they had to go through in leaving poverty-stricken

Ireland and scraping out a living in a new country. They just loved the life they were able to build in America, a middle-class existence in a wonderful country where hard work was its own reward. My mother came to this country in the early 1900s to live with an aunt. My father, Michael, was the oldest of three boys. At the age of 15, he was orphaned. Doing odd jobs, my father was not only able to get to America, but he helped to secure passage for his brothers, John and Patrick. This was the late 1800s.

The Greatest Generation

Tom Brokaw writes that my generation (the one that fought in World War II) was "The Greatest Generation." I disagree. My vote goes to my parents' generation. Growing up in Ireland, they had to make a decision. Should they stay and battle poverty throughout a lifetime, or break away and go to America, the land of opportunity? To choose the latter meant scrimping to save the ocean fare, leaving family and friends, and embarking on what many experienced to be a perilous voyage. Upon arrival, nothing would be handed to them— they had to work for it. The only advantage for the Irish immigrants was that they had no language barrier.

My father came to Boston at the age of 23. His first job was as a gardener in Brighton. Next he joined the Boston Elevated Railway. Back at the turn of the century, horses pulled the trolleys, and it was my father's job to take care of the unruly horses—a difficult chore at best. He soon decided the job wasn't for him and, looking for security, he joined the post office. Initially he was assigned to New York because he could join the force more quickly, and for a while the family lived in Harlem. He then transferred to Boston, and until his retirement at age 65, he was a letter carrier in Brighton.

I had two older brothers. John was born in 1908 and Jim in 1913. My mother took care of the home and did a fantastic amount of work. She did all of our laundry by hand and the follow-up ironing for a family of five. My mother prepared all the meals and washed the dishes; I don't think that any of the three boys even cleared the table. She baked all the bread we ate, and it was delicious, as was all her cooking. Of course, she did all the housework and shopping.

About a mile and a half away from our house was the focal point for the community, St. Columbkille's Catholic Church and school. I attended the parochial school from first grade through high school. The Sisters of St. Joseph did the teaching. They were backed up by a solid curate corps consisting of Fathers Desmond, Quinlan, Mack, and Callahan. When report cards were distributed, it was done by Monsignor Tracey, the pastor, or one of the curates. They would make pointed comments on the progress, or lack of progress, by a student. Discipline was firm but fair. I was an above-average student, so I usually passed muster. My favorite subject in grammar school was English. We worked hard at school, but I must say we didn't have to go home with the huge amount of homework that children have these days. With the exception of the years when I had piano lessons, from ages nine to 12, and time out for altar boy practice, my afternoons and weekends were devoted to play. Those were wonderful, carefree days.

Not many people on Falkland Street owned automobiles. You walked or rode the Boston Elevated Railway system (bus and street cars) wherever you wanted to go. Summertime demanded more mobility. In 1924, my father bought a used Model T Ford for $60. As a letter carrier, he must have walked about 12 miles a day, but he did not use the car to commute to work. His day began with about a two-mile walk to the Brighton Post Office. After delivering mail on his route all morning, he walked home for lunch and then had to return for an afternoon delivery. A walk home concluded his day.

My father was a staunch Irishman. He served as National Historian of the Hibernians. I remember once, in the late '30s, he urged me to enter an essay contest sponsored by the Hibernians: "Ireland's Contribution to the Making of America." I was busy with school and athletics, and as the deadline approached he became alarmed that I had not taken up the project. The next few days he spent busily composing an essay. He had it typed and entered in my name. It won second prize in the nationwide contest, $25. My prize received some publicity in the local paper.

However, when March 17 rolled around and the local Hibernians were looking for speakers for a program, there was a price to pay. It was suggested that I deliver my essay. Great idea for them—bad deal for me. I had to memorize the prose of my father. Somehow I got through the night. My debating experience in high school undoubtedly helped.

The First of Many Trips to Canada

For a summertime vacation, the family scheduled a trip to Canada in 1924. There were five of us: mother Bridget, father Michael, oldest son John—age 16 at the time—and James, 11. I was six. We visited Quebec (St. Anne de Beaupre), Montreal, a section of Ontario, and then came home. This was during Prohibition, but there wasn't any Prohibition in Canada. Approaching the border on our return, my parents put together a careful plot to smuggle a couple of bottles of whiskey.

Knowing we would be thoroughly searched, my mother fashioned an apron with two pockets in front to carry the bottles. Covering all was her cloth coat. Sure enough, at the Immigration stop, we were all asked to get out of the car and stand aside while the officers pulled the cushions out and thoroughly inspected everything. Given the OK, we returned and my mother, who was a teetotaler, was greatly relieved. That whiskey was much enjoyed during Sunday dinners. For guests who shared its taste, the story of how it was secured made it even more priceless. I never dreamed Canada would become a regular trek for me in my career.

For several other summers, we vacationed in the Sconticut Neck area of Fairhaven near Buzzards Bay at the southern entrance of the Cape Cod Canal. Rent for a cottage located about 75 yards from the water was $60 per month. I remember listening to rum runners maneuver at night in the bay. There didn't seem to be any restrictions on their operations. No one reported them, and no one chased them as they used a houseboat anchored in the bay to store the liquor.

I made my "stage debut" when I was in the seventh grade. A highlight of the Christmas season at St. Columbkille's was the annual presentation of the cantata. Without an audition, I was named to the role of third shepherd. I had one line: "All hail to Thee throughout all time." I was taken out of class to say it during a rehearsal presided over by Father William Desmond, one of the more popular curates. I had to say the line many times. How many ways can you say it? He grew exasperated and almost cancelled my participation. It was not a good start when your ultimate aim is a career as a radio sportscaster.

Somehow I got through the regular show, but I was not asked back the following year.

Time for Sports

When I was nine I started playing pick-up baseball in games sponsored by the park department. One of the big benefits of playing at the local parks was that you could attend major league baseball games for free. The Boston Braves sponsored a program called The Knot Hole Gang, where they gave children who played at the parks passes to the games. Public transportation to the Braves' Allston ball yard cost ten cents each way. This was the Great Depression, so on many an occasion, along with my friends, I walked the five miles to Braves Field.

We sat in the left-field pavilion. Below us was the Braves' bullpen. The visiting bullpen was in front of the right-field pavilion, and the grandstand was in between. Behind the right fielder was the Jury Box—seating about 1,000—and behind it was the scoreboard. The rest of the outfield had wooden bleacher seats atop a 15-foot high fence.

On our unmarked wooden plank seats, we got a perfect view of the home runs hit by Boston Braves star left fielder Walter Berger. He usually stroked high-arching balls. Sometimes they went over the fence and bleachers and onto the railroad tracks. Berger was a power hitter in an era when one-run baseball was the norm. Tall, handsome, non-controversial, he was our hero. His salary peaked at $12,000 a year. Today that salary would be $12 million a year. I thought so much of him that I took his name, Walter, at my Confirmation.

Pitching and defense were the keys to success in those days. If a game lasted more than two hours it had to have gone into extra innings. Except for Berger's accomplishments, the Braves were just an average team. Getting tickets to a game was never a problem—they went bankrupt in 1935. But if the attendance wasn't high, the all-around interest was considerable. *The* morning paper was the *Post,* and stories by Paul Shannon and Jack Malaney were given considerable play, along with cartoons by Bob Coyne.

On Sundays, there was usually a doubleheader at Braves Field. Admission was 50 cents. I sat in dead-center field and got a good line on the pitchers. Fred Frankhouse was one of my favorites. His curve and drop seemed to break five feet. In the center-field bleachers, we were too far away to hear the call of the starting lineups given by Braves announcer "Obie" O'Brien. Unamplified megaphone in hand, the portly O'Brien shouted out the names of the starting teams, first to the left-field bleachers, then to the third-base grandstand, then to the first-base grandstand, right-field pavilion, and finally to the jury box. I never recall him going into fair territory to inform those in the center-field bleachers. O'Brien became a folk hero. He was subject to a lot of kidding, which he took good-naturedly. Little did I think that 30 years later, I would be doing the public-address announcing for the Red Sox, without the burden of shouting into a megaphone.

After the game, it was autograph time. You had to be patient, but it seemed that all the players were cooperative. On one occasion, with several other youngsters, I accompanied right fielder Lance Richbourg up Babcock Street and across Commonwealth Avenue to the doorstep of his apartment near the field. It was baseball talk all the way. Afterward, some highly embellished stories were passed along to teammates and school chums.

The Red Sox, until Tom Yawkey took over in 1933, were an impoverished lot, but the pre-Yawkey team had a certain charm. Fenway Park had an embankment in front of its now celebrated left-field wall. Russ Scarritt was the left fielder who on occasion had to climb the hill to catch a fly. Visiting teams had many an adventure with the setup. In particular, Fatty Fothergill, a roly-poly outfielder of the Detroit Tigers, had some tough moments chasing fly balls. The hill must have been 10 feet high. It was angled sharply and not too well groomed.

In center field was a picket fence that was hazardous to friend and foe. A weak-hitting center fielder named Tom Oliver handled it rather well. Earl Webb was the Walter Berger of the Red Sox, although he was not a home-run hitter. His specialty was hitting doubles, and he set a league record at one time. It was tarnished by the fact that he never made a bid for a triple—he always stopped at second.

Those pre-Yawkey Red Sox were so bad that I never stayed for an autograph. I believe that the bleacher admission price was only 25 cents. In 1936, the Braves made a challenge for first place, and I recall a rare SRO (Standing-room-only) crowd of 36,000 at a Sunday doubleheader against the Giants. I was there.

My favorite sport, as a participant and a spectator, was hockey. I learned to skate at age 10. Most youngsters today are veteran players at that age. There was no problem finding ice—there were plenty of ponds and rivers. It was finding rinks. Fortunately, the winters were colder then, or at least they seemed to be. For several months each year, there was an opportunity to skate.

Usually I headed for Chandler's Pond, located about two miles from home. Saturdays were a particular treat. From eight in the morning until sunset, I would skate at Chandler's. There was no point in going home for lunch. It would have meant four miles more of walking. Unlike today's organized Pee Wees and Bantams, each player went at his own pace and we played pickup games on open ice—perfecting our skating skills traveling up and down the ice for hours. The game was informal, and the respective goals were fashioned from jackets and shoes piled on the ice. There was no goaltender, and there were no boards to frame a rink. Many times an errant pass slithered across the ice, and the puck wound up a hundred yards away. To minimize this occurrence, the art of stick handling was practiced by most of the boys. As new players arrived, they joined the game informally on one side or the other—sometimes there were as many as ten players on a side. There was very little body contact, and this form of casual play didn't really help develop our passing and shooting skills.

During extremely cold weather, the Charles River froze over. That meant a shorter walk—less than a mile—to gain a workout, but it could be particularly testing if there was a lot of wind. Many times near the end of the day spent on the Charles River near Watertown, we would skate down the river all the way to an area near Harvard Stadium, and then turn around and skate back to the Watertown area.

Public Speaking

Somehow, in the midst of the Depression, Monsignor Joseph Tracey, the pastor of St. Columbkille's, built the high school. I was a member of the first graduating class for boys in 1936. Emphasis was on college courses, Latin, Greek, English, general science, and math. It was during these years that I really started to develop my interest in public speaking as a member of the debate team. Luckily for my future career, St. Columbkille's fielded a strong team with regular competition against other Catholic schools. Our Greek teacher, Sister Denise, was also coach of the debating team. In her attempt to have the best team in the Catholic League, she prevailed upon James Foley, a 60-year-old English teacher at prestigious Boston Latin School, to attend our practice sessions to offer his critique and advice. It gave us an edge, and we won most of our debates.

I was also a member of the uniformed military cadet drill corps and a fife-and-drum marching band. Both appeared each March 17 in the South Boston St. Patrick's Day parade. Of course, I was also very involved in sports. The school sponsored baseball, football, and hockey teams, and I played on all three.

Early Broadcasting Influence

My interest in broadcasting goes way back. In 1930, when I was 12 years old, my friend from Brighton, Matthew Galligan, and I, somehow obtained tickets to a live network radio broadcast from the Hotel Bradford in Boston. It was the Blackstone Plantation program on CBS starring Julia Sanderson and Frank Crumit. The program was a musical variety show from a simulated plantation, where tobacco for Blackstone Cigars was grown. The announcer was Ed Herlihy, a Boston native and graduate of Boston College. I envied his job. His career flourished in New York as he became a well-known newsreel voice. Later I obtained tickets to a local live broadcast from the Salle Modern of the Statler Hotel in Boston. It was called the "I.J. Fox Fur Trappers" starring Buddy Clark singing popular songs of the day. Buddy later achieved national fame via records and network programs. Again, my focus was on the announcer, Frank Gallop. He went on to great success as a network voice.

When it came to announcers, the networks were full of them, all of them talented. Some did more than read the commercials—they became an integral part of the show. Don Wilson on the Jack Benny program drew almost as many laughs as Jack. Other memorable network voices belonged to Dan Seymour (he began at WNAC in Boston), Andre Baruch, Ben Grauer, Harry Von Zell, and Ford Bond. In Boston, the quality was high. John McNamara at WBZ, Ken Ovenden at WEEI, and several announcers at WNAC were among the best. At WNAC and the Yankee Network, Roland Winters (who later became Charlie Chan in the movies), and Vin Maloney were standouts.

Fred Hoey was one of my favorite baseball broadcasters. He had a long stint as the voice of the Red Sox and Braves in the 1920s and '30s. Hoey only announced home games, and when the Braves went on the road, he covered the Red Sox. Hoey was a home-team rooter, but he was genuine. His tenor-like delivery was upbeat, and he made the game come alive. Listeners might not have realized that when Fred acknowledged receipt of a warming cup of coffee from the concession stand, it was occasionally spiked with a drop or two of brandy. After all, those days were chilly when the east wind whipped in from the Charles River. His spirited delivery was what mattered. Hoey had a favorite player on the Braves—shortstop Rabbit Maranville—who was a colorful player. He always slid head first into a base, and in the field he could turn a pop fly into an event by making a vest-pocket catch. Hoey loved him, and I can still hear him cheering him on "Run, Rabbit, run," or "Slide, Rabbit, slide." Such partisanship would never do in today's sophisticated reports. It's hard to believe, but in those days the players left their gloves on the field when it came time for them to bat. On rare occasions, a batted ball would hit one of the gloves, but I never recall a player tripping over an opponent's glove.

In 1936, in answer to New Englanders' demands, Hoey was given a World Series assignment. While on the air, his voice failed and he could not continue. A couple of years later, in 1939, he was replaced by Frankie Frisch. He had been a superb ball player but had no experience in broadcasting. He had a poor voice and lasted only one year. WNAC made amends the next year, and smooth-voiced, talented Jim Britt was hired.

At WMEX, Boston, there was another great announcer, Win Elliot. He did sports and pretty much everything else. Elliot was a Boston native who had graduated from the University of Michigan. He had been a goaltender on their hockey team. He started in radio on WMEX in the '30s. WMEX began dabbling in sports so that Win's all-around announcing duties got him into that phase of radio. He had a rich, clear, tenor voice that enabled him to stay in broadcasting into his 80s with CBS radio.

To develop his skills, Win originated a program on WMEX called *Words With You*. It enabled him to develop his vocabulary, the very essence of an announcer's work. Over a 15-minute period, he simply took a list of words, probably culled from the daily newspaper, and expounded on them. He undoubtedly used something like the *Random House Dictionary of the English Language* as a source. He would give a word's varied meanings, its origin (often Latin), use it in a sentence, and then move on to another word. The practice stood him in good stead in a career lasting 60 years. Win could handle anything in broadcasting. His sports coverage ranged from baseball, boxing, horse racing, and hockey to CBS Sports Central on CBS radio. He was also the host of many game shows.

On the network level, Ed Thorgerson had an unforgettable voice. Deep, rich, authoritative—he became famous not only on radio but in newsreels as well. In 1966, when my family and I moved to Cape Cod, then-retired Ed Thorgerson turned out to be my next-door neighbor. Thorgerson's distinctive voice can still be heard in the Fox *Movietone* news and sports reports of the '30s and '40s. They are sometimes featured on the History Channel, The Learning Channel, and on A & E's *Biography*, as well as many other programs.

Thorgerson's career began in 1927 when he became an announcer at NBC in New York. He was in a field staffed by famous announcers—Jimmy Wallington, Frank Gallop, Ford Bond, Tiny Ruffner, Ed Herlihy, Don Wilson, and many others. Some of them became personalities in their own right, but most were straight-forward announcers. Versatility was the key for Thorgerson, and his rich, vibrant voice was a natural for the medium. He covered sports, news, special events, interviews, commercials, and dance band remotes—all in a day's work.

On March 1, 1932, it was Thorgerson reporting from a small country restaurant in Hopewell, New Jersey, who gave the first graphic account on NBC radio of the kidnapping of the 20-month-old son of Colonel Charles Lindbergh. It was a tragedy that stunned the nation. For the next 10 days and nights, his accounts kept the country—and via shortwave, the world—informed. It was one of *the* news stories of the 20th century.

In 1932, Thorgerson covered the winter Olympics at Lake Placid, New York. The star of the games, who won a gold medal in her specialty of figure skating, was Sonja Henie. Ed scooped the field with his interview of the "Queen of the Ice." After she retired from figure skating, Sonja went on to greater fame as a movie star with 20th Century Fox. Thorgerson left NBC the next year and turned to newsreels. With no television, his sports segment, matched with Lowell Thomas' news coverage for 20th Century Fox *Movietone News*, was seen on 17,000 theater screens. It was like having a constant audience of 60 million people. Thorgeson wrote his own scripts, and his incisive words and distinctive voice brought him countrywide recognition.

College football was the big sporting event of the '30s. Pro football, without the benefit of television coverage, had a limited appeal. *Movietone News* filmed all the major college games. Thorgerson devised the first Newsreel All-American football team. Other All-American teams were the creation of sportswriters and their friends and scouts. His gave visual proof of the high-level talent. It proved to be an instant hit.

When World War II broke out, he was shifted to *Movietone's* "World War" and "News of the Nation" newsreel departments. His powerful voice can be heard on many of those reports today. With the advent of television, Thorgerson brought his years of experience to *Newsreel Theater* and later a nightly newscast on WPIX, New York. Finally, he became an associate news director for the Dumont television network. Then he opted for retirement, next to me as it turned out, on Cape Cod.

There were no memoirs, no radio or television interviews, no speeches before Rotary Clubs. It was as though a switch had been clicked to the "off" position as far as his prominent career was concerned. The "on" position was turned to retirement. That meant golf at the Wianno Club and fishing in Nantucket Sound. During the winter months, he pursued the same sports in Florida. On occasion, his fishing companion was Ted Williams. It seemed incongruous to his family and friends that such a public figure could turn away from the spotlight so abruptly and totally. In truth, the path he followed in radio, television, and newsreels, demanded great craftsmanship in pressure-packed situations. Most of the radio and television programs were done live. There was no margin for error. In retirement, he kept hale and hearty with almost daily walks around Osterville. As Sinatra sang, "I did it my way." There may not be stories about his fascinating career, but the voice lives on.

A contemporary of Thorgerson, but not actually a rival in sports coverage, was Ted Husing, one of the finest play-by-play men in the broadcast of any sport. Graham McNamee was the original play caller, but his style was more colorful than factual. Husing, working for CBS, became the star. Thorgerson once told me how Husing, working alone, did a better job covering a regatta than four announcers on NBC. I recall Husing, again working alone, covering the National Doubles Tennis Tournament at the Longwood Cricket Club in Brookline, Massachusetts. For an entire Saturday afternoon, he made it informative and interesting. He could also be controversial. In 1935, he was banned from baseball broadcasts by Commissioner Judge K.M. Landis, because of his criticism of umpires.

In the mid-'30s, broadcasting a Harvard football game, he called the Crimson's quarterback Barry Wood "putrid." That ended his Harvard play-by-play career. But there were other sports he brought to life: America's Cup, the Kentucky Derby, golf, and college football. He wound up his career as a disc jockey in New York—a sad end to a brilliant career. But his legend lived on.

All the great broadcasters of the 1920s and 1930s influenced me as a youngster in my future career. After a pickup baseball game or hockey scrimmage, there was nothing better than to come home and listen to a game on the radio.

CHAPTER FOUR

College and the Navy

It was the beginning of my sophomore year at Northeastern University in Boston, and hockey-wise things were not going well. In my first year, I had not only made the freshman team, but had played almost 60 minutes of every game. To my surprise, when I tried out for varsity, I did not make the roster. Still, I hung in. I was allowed to practice with the team in my own makeshift uniform. We were scheduled to play against Brown, and my persistence paid off. One of the regulars could not play in the game.

I was given a uniform, and halfway through the first period I got a chance to play. I was a left-hand shot playing right wing. Very soon, I got the puck. Starting at our blue line, I put on a burst of speed and got by one of their forwards. As I approached their left defenseman, I was able to crank it up some more and go wide around him. Bearing in on the goal, I shifted to a forehand and drilled a hard shot high into the net, just inside the right post. The team went on to a victory, and I was a regular thereafter.

In retrospect, it was kind of a "Rocky" moment—the undervalued underdog makes the big play. Maybe I should say it was a "Rocket" moment. Rocket Richard, a left-hand shot who played right wing for the Canadiens, later made that type of goal famous.

Between graduation from high school in 1936 and going to Northeastern, I had gotten other sports experiences under my belt. I was a catcher for the Brighton Civics in the top-rated Boston Park League. About a dozen teams represented various areas of the city and the rosters ranged from high school players to some players who were in their 30s. Because it was twilight play, the games were limited to seven innings or less. I was not a great success. I could handle the pitchers all right, but my hitting was weak.

That turned out to be the only season I played in the major Park League. We played four nights a week, and the games were well attended. During the playoffs, some of the games would draw as many as 4,000 fans.

Northeastern and Eddie Barry

Northeastern had a five-year course, with the last four years featuring the co-operative, work-study plan. For freshmen, the year was spent in studies, and of course playing the sports that you qualified for. I played three: football, hockey, and baseball. This was a time when freshmen had their own teams and were not allowed to participate in varsity sports.

The hockey schedule was modest. We played other freshman teams as well as prep schools like Exeter and Andover. My defense partner was Lew Cunningham, who lived in Lincoln, Massachusetts. He commuted to school in an old Chevy that chugged along in all kinds of weather. Our practice time at the Boston Arena was 6:15 a.m. every Monday, Wednesday, and Friday. Lew would pick me up at 5 a.m. each practice morning. In all four years, we never missed a workout.

Once they let me on the varsity team, my skills improved. I was a right wing playing with Johnny Chipman and Eddie Barry. I scored five goals in games against Bowdoin, and later against M.I.T. This was not entirely due to my own talent. For most of the goals, it was the passing and playmaking of Barry and Chipman that set them up. Chipman was a former All-Star forward at Arlington High School, and Barry was an All-Star at Wellesley High School. They had played in the two best leagues in the State—the Greater Boston Interscholastic, and the Bay State League. I was the pond skater from Brighton.

Eddie Barry played later with the Boston Olympics. Following the war (he had been in the Coast Guard), he was called up to the Boston Bruins in 1946 and played in 19 games. That was a tremendous accomplishment for that time because the National Hockey League coaches and executives did not think that American players could perform up to the standards of their league. Later Barry returned to the Olympics and closed out his career as a coach. He turned his efforts to golf, worked diligently at the game, and 12 times became the club champion at the Charles River Country Club in Newton, Massachusetts. Charles River was, and is, a championship course. It has hosted PGA events, as well as many Massachusetts amateur tournaments. In 1967, he won the New England Amateur championship, and in 1981, he won the New England Senior Amateur title. Nationally he qualified four times for the United States Golf Association Senior Amateur, and twice he was the Massachusetts

Senior Champion (1979 and 1981). In 1966, he won the Tournament of Club Champions. His amateur victories were so numerous that the Charles River Country Club members had a bronze plaque placed on a huge rock at the front of the clubhouse and inscription reading, "In honor of Edward Barry who proudly represented CCRC at the highest level of amateur competition for over forty years."

Father Joe

Another pond skater who made it onto his college team was Joe Maguire. Joe was a very close friend while we both attended St. Columbkille's High School. He was a year behind me, but we shared a mutual interest in sports. He lived quite close to the school and adjacent to McKenney Playground where baseball, football, and hockey were played. For the latter, the field was flooded during the winter months, and for me it was much handier than making the trek to Chandler's Pond. The high school football team worked out and played some games at McKenney's. Joe Maguire was a quarterback, and for the baseball season he played shortstop. Hockey was our big interest, but we did not have the benefit of playing on rinks.

Following graduation, Joe went to Boston College. Joe's ambition was to make the Eagles hockey team, but the odds were not favorable. Boston College was a hockey powerhouse led by John "Snooks" Kelly, the legendary coach. He had started the hockey program in 1933, and while there were limited practice facilities, he generally recruited the best high school players around. He disdained securing Canadian players. He could fill out a squad with Greater Boston All-Stars. When Joe Maguire enrolled in 1938, he was joined by three All-Stars from the Greater Boston Interscholastic League—Ray Chaisson and Al Dumond—who were high-scoring forwards from Rindge Tech, and Bob Mee a flashy defenseman from Arlington High School. Coach Kelley put another power forward, John Pryor, from Framingham High School and the Bay State Hockey League, at right wing with Chaisson and Dumond.

Although Joe Maguire was just a pond skater, he soon displayed a talent for steady play on defense. He proved to be an excellent choice to pair with Bob Mee. In the 1939–1940 season, the Eagles finished with a record of 12 wins, five losses, and a tie. Chaisson led the way in scoring with 33 goals. In the 1940–1941 season, Boston College had 13 wins and only one loss. Chaisson had 29 goals in the 14 games. Game in and game out, Joe Maguire was a consistent performer as the first-string left defenseman. It was quite an accomplishment for the young man from St. Columbkille's. His lack of rink experience didn't prove to be a handicap at all.

Following graduation, Joe very quietly decided on the priesthood, and he enrolled in St. John's Seminary just down the street from Boston College. After ordination, he served in a variety of parishes and assignments and was later appointed an assistant to Cardinal Cushing. Under Cushing's successor, Humberto Cardinal Medeiros, Monsignor Maguire became his secretary and later was named Auxiliary Bishop of Boston. In 1977, he became Bishop of Springfield, retiring in 1991. He is now Bishop Emeritus of Springfield. His has been a richly rewarding life, nurtured on religion, but with golden memories of sports in the background.

With the benefit of television, he became a Boston Bruins fan, and we have kept in touch through the years. One year, with the Bruins playing the Whalers, he made the short trip to Hartford, and

I had him as a guest on the telecast. I made sure to recall those triumphant days at Boston College. One thing was proven by the interview—the Bishop was right at home in a hockey arena.

Copy Boy

After the first full year of going to school at Northeastern University, students came under the cooperative plan. The idea was that for ten weeks you would go to school, and the next ten weeks would be spent at a job that ideally would tie in with your studies and ambition. In my case, the school had just started an alliance with *The Boston Globe*. Copy boys were needed in the editorial and advertising departments. I was assigned to the latter. The first thing I remember was $10.88—my net pay each week. The gross was $12. It was 1938, and it was my first real job. I had spent my leisure time in pursuit of sports, and had carefully avoided any kind of work. Growing up caddying would have been the most natural, but I never went near the Commonwealth Country Club in Newton as my brothers had.

I was proud of the *Globe* job because I wore a suit to work. For some reason I didn't care for jobs that required you to wear a uniform. Maybe it was because my father wore one as a letter carrier, and I hoped to avoid that employment, as well as that of policeman, fireman, and Boston Elevated Railway worker. When I got on the bus each morning, heading for my *Globe* job, I could have been a young banker, broker, or junior executive on the move. I did not take my lunch in order to keep up the image. I ate at Thompson's Spa on Washington Street opposite the *Globe* and sat next to the very bankers, brokers, and other executives I was trying to emulate. A full lunch could be purchased for 35 cents.

My dream of having an executive-type job was shattered when my first daily assignment was to carry the rolls to department stores such as Jordan Marsh, Whites, Filenes, Gilchrists, and others. They were the *Globe's* biggest advertisers. The rolls were copies of that day's *Boston Globe* rolled up into cylinders of various sizes. They were awkward to carry, but more importantly to me, it was embarrassing to be seen with them. Perched precariously on my shoulder, the rolls were tell-tale evidence that I had nothing more than an entry-level job.

Larry Healy was boss of the copy boys, and Bob Warren, Eddie Carr, Paul Connell, and Charley Spencer were in the group. The display desk, which coordinated the entire operation, was run by Bill O'Connell. The sales force included Jack Hamilton—a real favorite since he handled the movies and theatres and gave out passes. Others were Tim Desmond, Jack O'Connell, Frank McCarthy, Bill Bailey, Ted Poole, and Jim McCarrick. The chief honcho was Andy Dazzi, who had close connections at City Hall and the State House. Down front was classified advertising and Harold Delaney, Howie Flanagan, Clif Keane, and others handled the customers. Mike Lewis was out in front of the *Globe* all day, selling papers and booking numbers.

This was Newspaper Row—a fascinating place on Washington Street in downtown Boston. There was the *Boston Post*, the *Globe* and just as I arrived, the last days of the *Boston Transcript*. The *Globe's* building was hardly modern, but it was not as rickety and unstable as the *Post's*.

Election day was the most interesting, and the *Globe* made a fetish of predicting returns. Not having an alliance with radio, the *Globe's* returns were posted on a chalkboard in the front of the building. Reporter John Barry was to change the relationship with radio. A mustachioed, dapper man with a good voice, he had a nightly 15-minute program on WBZ radio, fully sponsored by Shawmut Bank. I never spoke to him, but since I thought radio announcers, news reporters, and sports reporters were the epitome of fame, I felt honored to be working on the same paper as John Barry. Several on the *Globe* staff had their own claim to fame. Joe Dineen, James Powers, and Louis Lyons were among them. And the *Boston Post* had the most famous of all—Bill Cunningham. Hockey reigned supreme as *the* sport in the '30s. Victor Jones, the *Globe*'s sports editor, who later became the managing editor, would cover games in person. He was joined by Gerry Moore, Tom Fitzgerald, Herb Ralby, and Harold Kaese.

I guess it was a promotion, but somewhere along the line I became an office boy for W. O. Taylor, the owner of the *Globe*, and his son Davis Taylor. It really meant I was working for their secretary, Miss Theresa Buckley. It got me out of carrying the rolls. W. O. was kindly, gracious, and a wonderful gentleman. His son Davis was cut from the same mold.

Politics

Politics was second nature to the Boston Irish. Although I've never been interested in public office myself, in 1940 I decided to try to talk my father into running for office. He had to take mandatory retirement at age 65 from the post office. He was mentally sharp and in tremendous physical shape from walking all those miles for all those years. I felt that somehow he should stay active. Why not run for state representative? He had spent a lifetime helping other people as a member of the Hibernians, the St. Vincent DePaul Society, and the Knights of Columbus. As a native of Galway, he had been particularly active in Irish affairs. The Ward 22 district was replete with first- and second-generation Irish. It took a lot of persuasion, but he finally agreed. Our budget was limited, but we managed to order up some banners with CUSICK prominently displayed. We held house parties. That's how you campaigned in those days. My father did a good job as the main speaker. I remember that he once introduced Boston Mayor James Michael Curley at an Irish games celebration in Hyde Park.

The competition was Charles Artesani, a Boston College graduate and a lawyer. Artesani had gotten attention by sponsoring a baseball team in the Boston Park League. Scores and standings with his name attached were published in the Boston papers all summer long. It gave him strong name recognition. As it turned out, the team made him the winner. My father took the loss graciously, and Artesani went on to a distinguished career in the legislature and eventually was made a judge.

In 1941, my father was contacted by Thomas Eliot, who was running for Congress in the Ninth Congressional District that included Ward 22. The sprawling ninth district—later represented by John F. Kennedy in his first step in politics, and after that by Tip O'Neill, the famous House Speaker—was heavily populated by Irish Americans. Eliot, a patrician Yankee, son of the famous Harvard University President Charles Eliot, sought guidance on reaching the majority population in the district—the Irish. Eliot came to our house for a discussion of what he should do to appeal to them. My father gave him guidance and worked diligently for his election. He won but only served a two-year term. He went on to become chancellor of St. Louis University.

Broadcasting and Soap

As I had worked to get my father elected, my parents also supported my career aspirations, after a fashion. In 1941, when I was still at Northeastern, I talked my way into an announcing job at a 250-watt radio station, WCOP. The station was located in the Copley Plaza Hotel in Boston. It signed off at sunset after broadcasting an array of programming that in no way matched the elegance of the hotel. A raucous "Farmer Russ" handled the morning shift with stories that weren't funny and music that was indiscriminate. The rest of the day had an assortment of man-in-the-street interviews, news, and music of every description. The studios and offices were jammed into a couple of rooms in the mezzanine of the hotel. The news ticker was located in the bathtub of the men's room. That situation provided some interesting moments when nature's call and scheduled newscasts overlapped.

I persuaded the general manager, A.N. "Bud" Armstrong, that I should do a nightly sportscast beginning April 1, when, with the coming of spring, the station's allotted broadcast time expanded to 6 p.m. I was inspired by the launching of a broadcast career by Tom Harmon—the All-America halfback from Michigan. After graduating, he joined a network as a sportscaster for ABC radio. My picture had been published in *The Boston Globe* sports section along with a brief story summing up my hockey career. I thought that, in a way, I was a smaller edition of Harmon, and Armstrong was persuaded. There was no mention of money. Armstrong simply didn't have it in his budget, and I knew that I could secure press passes to Fenway Park and Braves Field. That would more than compensate me.

Shortly after the programs started, a salesman for WCOP sold Lindbrook Clothiers—a men's shop on Washington Street in Boston—on the idea of sponsoring a five-minute nightly scoreboard program. Lindbrook wanted to corner the tie market in Boston. Each person buying a tie would be able to fill out an entry blank. There would be a drawing, and the winner would receive an all-expenses-paid trip to New York City. I did the program, and again, no talent fee was mentioned. The broadcast had been on about a week when my mother made the long trek from Brighton to Boston. She bought a tie at Lindbrooks, took an entry blank, and told the salesman what a fine program they were sponsoring. After a couple of weeks, it was time to pick a winner. There was only one problem. There were no entries. A befuddled Lindbrook man spoke up: "I don't understand it, I sold a tie to a woman who took an entry blank. Where is it?" Needless to say, the program was cancelled, but that didn't affect my nonexistent income.

In 1941, I left the *Globe* and worked a midnight-to-8 a.m. shift at Lever Brothers, a soap manufacturer, in Cambridge. With the advent of World War II, I knew I would be in the service soon, so I was looking for the most money I could get. When I finally went into the service, I had not gone directly from my job at the *Globe*. The paper, however, treated me like an employee, and during my three-and-a-half years of service, I received their newsletter and other goodies regularly. I don't know who was responsible for it, but it was most welcome. It was a touch of class that typified *The Boston Globe*, and that class was one of the reasons that the paper became No. 1 in the market.

Lever Brothers paid $37 per week—more than my father was making in the post office. It was grueling work, standing beside a conveyor belt studded with cakes of Swan Soap. My job was to place a small cake of Swan onto a larger one. It was tedious. That, along with my job at WCOP, meant that I didn't get much sleep.

A Talent for Public Speaking

Beside sports and my 'jobs,' I also participated in Northeastern's annual public speaking contest. Since I had been a member of the debating team at St. Columbkille's High School, I entered the competition. The contestant had to prepare a 10-minute presentation on any subject, and deliver it without notes. There were several preliminary rounds until four finalists were selected. They spoke before a school assembly at Jordan Hall. In four of the five years I was at the school, I participated. I reached the finals each year, won two years, and finished second in the other two years.

One year, my subject was "Problems in Defense." My closing statement was an eloquent plea "for the United States to build a strong defense to preserve the last light of democracy left shining in the world." It was a line I borrowed from the actor Joel McCrea in the movie *Foreign Correspondent*. It was a winner. The $40 first prize came in handy, and I was delighted that my father was in the audience. The speeches were to be ten minutes in length, but in all my qualifying talks, and in the finals at Jordan Hall, I never went beyond eight. I was never disqualified, and it kept judges and students from dozing off. I've always felt it is important to be short, sharp, and focused in public speaking.

90-Day Wonder

At age 23—the same age as my father when he came to America—it was time to go out into the world. I joined the Navy right after Pearl Harbor. I was sworn in January 1942, and allowed to finish school, graduating from Northeastern University the following June. It seemed natural for me to join the Navy. My brother John—ten years older than I—had trained for the sea as a cadet on the USS *Nantucket*. The maritime industry had suffered severely during the Depression, and in the 1930s he scrambled for employment in civilian life. With the war's outbreak, he returned to the sea and pursued a long life as a captain of ships all over the world. Before retirement, he was port captain of the Panama Lines in Haiti. My brother Jim was married with two children, and he was employed as a shipbuilder at the Navy Yard in Charlestown.

While completing my senior year at Northeastern, I enrolled in the Navy's V 12 program. It was open to college graduates and consisted of two weeks of indoctrination and three months of intense study of navigation, gunnery, and seamanship. Upon completion you were a commissioned officer. "Ninety Day Wonders" we were called. I was called to service in August 1942. My indoctrination was at Notre Dame for two weeks, and the next three months were spent grinding away at Tower Hall at the downtown Chicago campus of Northwestern University. I never studied so hard—failing was not an option for me.

After being made an ensign, I was assigned to the Sub Chaser Training Center in Miami, Florida. I completed a two-month course and was assigned to the USS *SC450*, based in Key West, Florida. My ship was the second wood-hull sub chaser built by the American Car and Foundry Co. It had been commissioned on May 2, 1940, about two years before I was commissioned.

Four-hundred thirty-eight sub chasers were built during the war. They served in all of the theaters of action—manned mostly by reservists like me. They were 110 feet long with a 15-foot beam. Armament was a dozen depth charges, two 20-millimeter guns amidships, and a three-inch 23-gun forward (or a 40-millimeter gun). The crew consisted of 24 men and three officers.

The *SC450* and two other sub chasers were formed into a division operating with the Fleet Sonar School that trained other officers in sonar techniques. Old S-class submarines would practice elusive maneuvers, and the sub chasers, manned by the students, would practice tracking routines. Most of the trainees would go on to become sonar officers aboard a variety of ships: destroyers, patrol craft, and sub chasers.

In addition to being a school ship, the *SC450* patrolled the east coast of Florida, portions of the Gulf of Mexico, and the shipping lanes between Cuba and the Florida Keys. But basically we were in port and tied up each day at about 4 p.m. (or, as we say in the Navy, 1600 hours).

The submarines we maneuvered with were of World War I vintage. Some of the sub officers would invite us to go with them to see how the other side worked. Some of my fellow officers went, but the idea never appealed to me. My instincts were confirmed one day when one of the subs, which had been running on the surface, suddenly slipped beneath the waves and never came up. Only the people who had been on the open bridge survived. We spent days searching for the sub with no success.

The director of the Sound School was Captain Joseph Keating, a Boston native. At a meeting in the officers' club, he asked me about playing baseball. Key West had a huge amount of military activity. One of the main recreational activities was a baseball league comprised of the Sound School, the Naval Base, the Naval Air Station, and the Army. Enlisted men made up the rosters, but one officer was allowed to play for each team. Most likely due to my experience as a catcher for the Brighton Civics in the Boston Park League (perhaps Keating had seen me play), I wound up as a catcher for Sound School, playing two nights a week. In all, I served 21 months in Key West.

Captain Cusick

Later, I was handed my first command as captain of the USS *SC1322* operating out of Norfolk, Virginia. We were an escort for a variety of convoys around Cape Hatteras to Morehead City, North Carolina. It was the roughest duty I had in the war. The waves were mountainous and the sub chaser was tossed around like a cork in the ocean. After a couple of months, I was sent to Plymouth, England, to take over command of another sub chaser, the 1355. This was after D-Day. The ship provided escort duty between Plymouth, England, and LeHavre, France. Our job was to shepherd convoys overnight to France, remain there during the day, and return the next night. It was routine work, but one night we got a surprise. I was in my cabin and suddenly heard a large Boom! I thought, "This is it." I ran on deck. No enemy. It turned out that one of the other escort's depth charges had somehow gotten loose, rolled off the stern and exploded.

This escort work lasted three months until the end of the war. We were sent back to the United States for a complete overhaul to ready us for service in the Pacific. But the atom bomb ended the conflict.

Your Navy Reporter

In 1946, when I was waiting for enough points to be discharged from the Navy, I was stationed at the public information office at the First Naval District back home in Boston. It was March. I noticed that one of the small aircraft carriers located in Boston awaiting reassignment was named the USS *Shamrock Bay*. My father was an avid student of Irish history and that country's contribution to America. He was a longtime member of the Ancient Order of Hibernians.

I thought, why not have the Hibernians present a gift to the captain of the *Shamrock Bay* on March 17—Saint Patrick's Day? It would be good PR for the Navy and the Hibernians. My father was delighted. He secured a shillelagh for $10, had a scroll prepared, and had the Irish consul in Boston invited to the ceremony. The event was broadcast live by the Yankee network, and the *Boston Post* had a front page, four-column picture of the ceremony. The ship's captain, James Leeper, graciously accepted the honors. In his speech, he was careful not to mention the fact that while the ship had an Irish-sounding name, it was actually named for Shamrock Bay, Alaska.

I persuaded my boss, Captain John Harrigan, to let me originate a radio program and interview some of the personnel who were being released. With his blessing, I contacted WHDH, located in the Hotel Touraine in Boston. WHDH was, to put it mildly, an undistinguished radio station. One of its programs featured reports on fish arrivals at the ports of Boston and Gloucester, Massachusetts. The station had no problem allowing me to host a program known as *Your Navy Reporter*. It was on in the mid-afternoon of one day a week. I would simply look over the list of people to be discharged and select the most prominent and set up the interview. Bill Sullivan, later the founder of the New England Patriots, was one of my guests on the program.

At this time, a friend of mine from Brighton, John Ryan, persuaded me to join the Joseph Kennedy Post VFW. He had known young Joe in the service and had greatly admired him. Kennedy had been killed in a secret mission over the English Channel. After joining the organization, Ryan suggested that I interview Joe Kennedy's brother, Jack, who was going to run for Congress in the Ninth District, which, of course, included Brighton.

I did the interview. I have no recollection of its content, but it must have been about his war career and candidacy. At that time, Kennedy was just starting his political career. He had earned a reputation as a war hero for *PT-109* but I remember him as pitifully thin and an awkward public speaker. Jack Kennedy gave no indication to me that he would someday be president of the United States.

I was separated from the U.S. Naval service in March 1946. I had served three years, five months, and 25 days of active duty. Like most veterans I was looking forward to finally starting my real life. I felt lucky to be starting my career, but I couldn't help but think of some of my childhood friends who did not make it back home.

CHAPTER FIVE

Behind the Mike

After I got out of the Navy, I worked briefly at a radio station on Cape Cod, then got a job as a staff announcer at WBET in Brockton, Massachusetts. My salary was $55 per week. Five days a week, I put in eight-hour shifts. A shift included serving as the disc jockey for a program called *Turntable Terrace*. News was reported on the hour. The material was taken from the Associated Press news ticker. Although the station was owned by the Brockton Enterprise, neither the newspaper, nor its staff, provided any news.

Rocky

I persuaded the program director to let me broadcast sports. During the school season, there was Brockton High football and basketball. What to do in the summer? An eight-team Old Colony Baseball League played for the fun of it on Saturday afternoons. Brockton's representative was the Ward Two Memorial team, and I broadcast their games. The catcher? Rocco Marchegiano. His dream of being a major league catcher had been shattered by an arm injury. It had happened while he was playing baseball in the service. For a lark, he had attempted to pitch, but the strain proved too much. He later tried out with the Chicago Cubs farm team in Fayetteville, North Carolina. There was no demand for a weak-throwing catcher. But that right arm was to lead him to glory in another sport.

For Ward Two Memorial he was the cleanup hitter, and three or four hits a game was the norm for him. Attendance at those games was limited to relatives, friends, and me. I sat in the stands and did play-by-play.

I next met Rocky in the fall of 1947 when Gene Caggiano, a Brockton mechanic who was serving as his manager, brought the now renamed Rocky Marciano to WBET for an interview. They were promoting a local boxing show featuring the young slugger. It was a brief, and not exactly memorable, chat. Rocky then moved seriously into boxing, and in a short time he scored four straight knockouts in Providence. He changed managers and signed with Al Weill.

I was never Marciano's close friend or confidant, but I knew Rocky. I met him two more times. Our paths next crossed on September 23, 1952. I was to be the new Bruins announcer, and Rocky was battling "Jersey Joe" Walcott for the heavyweight championship of the world at Philadelphia's Veteran Stadium. I was invited by the Bruins to their training camp at Hershey, Pennsylvania, to be followed by a stop at Philadelphia to watch the fight. I did not have a ringside seat, but from where I was, I could plainly see that Rocky was losing the fight to the more skillful Walcott. Marciano had reached the summit against improbable odds. He was 23 1/2 years old before he really began to fight. He was not tall, had a short reach and a somewhat clumsy and awkward style. But as in baseball—he could hit. With a devastating punch, he knocked out Walcott.

I was invited—along with the Boston writers, family, and supporters—to his hotel suite after the fight. Rocky was lying on a bed. His nose, near his left eye, was sliced; his face was battered. The only question I had: "If this is the winner, what does the loser look like?" There were copious tears from his siblings. The entire scene was hardly a joyous celebration. He was to be the champion for a little more than three and a half years. He retired undefeated in 1957.

His retirement drew protests from Al Weill. Their relationship was tenuous at best, and Marciano felt that his arrangement with Weill had cost him dearly. Many thought that Marciano, once he got out of the clutches of Weill, would return to the ring. He never did. He spent his time with his family, making personal appearances, and watching his investments.

In the early '60s, I was producing and hosting a program on Channel 5, which appeared before Red Sox baseball. It was called, *The Dodge Boys Remember,* and each week it featured a sports personality who was a legend in the New England area. Rocky was the highest on the list and he came. He brought his film of the sensational victory over Walcott. His talent fee? $150. It was well within budget. Rocky was congenial, articulate, and certainly made the program one of the best in the series.

He died at age 46 in a plane crash in 1969. His tragic ending took a good man from the sports scene. Marciano reached the top of the boxing world on his own terms—with honesty, integrity, and hard work. His character shone throughout his impeccable career.

The direction of my own career in broadcasting after the war also took some turns. Being a sports announcer hoping to make the major leagues was a kind of a gypsy life, albeit, in my case, one confined to eastern Massachusetts.

Before joining WBET, it had been hard to find a job. After I was discharged from the Navy, I found that those who had pre-war broadcasting jobs had to be rehired, and new stations were not up to speed in their construction effort. Answering an advertisement in *Broadcasting Magazine,* I found a job with WOCB, a 250-watt station owned by the *Cape Cod Standard Times.* The job was to broadcast three newscasts a day at 8:15 a.m., noon, and 6 p.m. Material for the broadcasts was culled from the paper's news desk. In between newscasts, I sold ads and serviced the accounts. I must confess, that when the summer months rolled around, I spent a fair amount of the daytime hours at Craigville Beach. I never missed an assignment, though. My pay was $32 per week. My housing, in an elegant private home on Lewis Bay in Hyannis, was just $5 a week.

My goal at WOCB was to develop sports programming. I talked the general manager into letting me broadcast the tennis matches of touring pros. Two of them were Welby Van Horn, and Bobby Riggs. In the early '70s, when he was long over the hill, Riggs hustled his way into a nationally televised match with Billie Jean King, an outstanding female player who decisively defeated him as 37 million watched. Riggs and Van Horn were displaying their skills at the nearby Oyster Harbors Club. Even for top players it was a scrambling life, and they were hardly drawing enough fans to provide meal money. Still, the experience gave me background to do broadcasts of the National Doubles Tournament at the Longwood Cricket Club in Brookline and later to handle some *BostonLobsters* telecasts on TV38.

Luck stayed with me that summer. One September evening, a friend from Brighton, John Hurley, introduced me to beautiful

Barbara Mullin of Brookline, Massachusetts. Barbara was a fourth-grade school teacher in Wellesley, Massachusetts, and was working as the hostess at Bill Cox's Sea Grille on Cape Cod. Several days later, Barbara was walking down Main Street in Hyannis and spotted me doing one of my daily newscasts from my WOCB storefront location. When my broadcast was finished, I asked her for a date. After Labor Day, I moved to the new job at WBET. Barbara went back to Wellesley, about 50 miles away. We continued to date regularly through the fall, were engaged at Christmas, and married the following June.

While at WBET, I heard that the minor league Springfield Indians were looking for a broadcaster, and I auditioned. If a third-place finish was any consolation—that's where I finished. Herb Carneal, who went on to have a great career in Minneapolis, was the winner. Bob Delaney, who later became a Red Sox announcer, was second.

The Irish Hour

After spending a year and a half at WBET, I answered an ad in *Broadcasting Magazine* looking for a sports announcer for a new station—WVOM. It was licensed to Brookline, next door to Boston. On the plus side, its 5,000 watts covered a wide area of Greater Boston and beyond. On the negative side, its position—1600 on the dial—meant that anyone who owned a radio manufactured before World War II couldn't receive it. WMEX was at 1510 on the AM dial and that was about the limit for reception of stations on the right side of the radio dial. Nonetheless, I hand-delivered my resume and a tape of my work to the Brookline home of the general manager, Ben Bartzoff. I got the job, and the three years I spent with the station turned out for me to be Broadcasting 101. It was good timing. With the birth of our daughter, Martha, in 1948, I needed to make more money and move forward with my career to support my young family.

Much of the WVOM's programming was oriented towards foreign language speakers. Three hours a day, from 11 a.m. to 2 p.m., we broadcast *The Italian Hour*. Other languages, cultures, and countries were also taken aboard. For sports, I did a nightly 15-minute roundup, but there was no sponsor. So, to earn my keep, I joined the frustrated sales staff. I noticed that there was no *Irish Hour* in the station's lineup and started one by hosting a one-hour presentation Sunday nights at 8 p.m. In searching for a sponsor, I made a call on Bill Shields, owner of Shields Electric Company on Franklin Street in Boston, and I sold him on the idea of *The Irish Hour*. He had appliances to sell, especially television sets, and he tentatively sponsored the Sunday night *Irish Hour*.

The program began attracting listeners, but more importantly it attracted live talent. Irish bands and singers supplemented the recordings. The orchestras of Tommy Shields and Jack Sullivan were happy with the exposure, and popular Irish recording star Connie Foley was a regular. To say the program was an instant success is putting it mildly. Soon, *The Irish Hour* was on seven nights a week, and Shields was sponsoring the program every night, and for good reason. He was selling television sets as fast as he could stock them. It was obvious that his customers—some who traveled from 20, 30, and 40 miles away—were Irish. Their brogues could be heard throughout the store as they thanked him for his sponsorship of their favorite radio program. Our records were compliments of E. O'Byrne DeWitt, who owned a store in Roxbury. His travel agency in the same location was a thriving business.

In all of my years in broadcasting, I have never been associated with a program so successful in converting advertising into sales. Television sets at that time cost $700–$800, a lot of money in the '40s. While Shields usually made a credit arrangement with his downtown customers (and also gave generous discounts), he was delighted to see that his newly found Irish customers generally paid cash.

Proof of the popularity of *The Irish Hour* was the appearance of the legendary mayor of Boston, James Michael Curley, on the program. In 1949, the show originated live from Hibernian Hall in Roxbury. Before a packed house, with the broadcast well underway, he made his appearance with a slow walk down the center aisle to the stage. The delayed entry was a hallmark of Curley's political strategy. As the plaudits died down, he gave an engaging speech on Irish history. In 1950, when he was making a political comeback, we gave him 15 minutes, from 7:45 to 8 p.m., just before *The Irish Hour* on Sunday nights to talk on any subject he wanted. It was usually Irish history. He delivered it flawlessly without notes or a script. He had to climb a flight of stairs to enter the studio, and you could see that physically he was slipping, but his mind was as sharp as ever. In 1952, he appeared on the program to endorse the Democratic candidate for president, Adlai Stevenson. Curley knew the impact of *The Irish Hour*.

At WVOM, I broadcast all kinds of sports: high school and college football, basketball, hockey, the National Tennis Doubles from the Longwood Cricket Club in Brookline, and the state amateur golf tournament. I covered the Boston Olympic hockey team of the Eastern League. Ben Bartzoff, the general manager, and I had a simple agreement—I could broadcast any sport or sporting event on

WVOM, as long as it did not cost him any money. If the event was sponsored, so much the better.

Ed Stanky

At WVOM, I had to scramble. One program idea I came up with depended on Ed Stanky's broken leg. Any history of the Boston Braves would include more than a line or two about Stanky. As second baseman, he played on the pennant-winning team of 1948. Small in stature, Stanky was not a fast runner, but he could get on base one way or another. If a walk was needed, he could foul off pitches all day, until he got one. He attempted to distract hitters by playing near second base and waving his arms until umpires forbade the practice. He followed the dictum of his one-time manager Leo Durocher: "Nice guys finish last."

Early in August 1948, Stanky, who was having a terrific year as lead-off man, broke his leg. At the time, he partnered a formidable double-play combination with the talented Alvin Dark. It was a crushing blow to the Braves. Stanky was taken to St. Elizabeth's Hospital in Brighton. A couple of miles away, at our WVOM studios in Brookline, I had an idea. Since Stanky would be immobilized for a month or more, why not get him to do a nightly sportscast on WVOM? It would take his mind off his injury, keep him involved in the game, and he could make some money. How much, I didn't know. I visited him in the hospital and made my proposition. He was very interested, and we reached a critical moment. How much was he worth?

To my surprise, he knew how much Jimmy Foxx, one of the game's greatest hitters and a retired Red Sox first baseman, had made in the early 1940s when WEEI—a radio powerhouse—hired him. Foxx had agent Jimmy Silin, who negotiated a $500-a-week contract. Stanky asked for $100 per program! It was far more than we thought we could afford. Whatever the sum, however, I would have to get a sponsor, and $500 a week was far more than any advertiser (except Shields) was spending on the station. I dejectedly went back to WVOM and decided to give it one shot. I contacted Ed Baker, of Baker Ford, one of New England's largest Ford dealers. They were located right around the corner from WVOM, at Brookline Village.

As a baseball fan, Baker warmed to the idea of an association with Stanky via a nightly 15-minute program. The only problem was he didn't have any cars to sell. Three years after the war had ended, Ford Motor Company was not up to full speed. The cars that they manufactured were quickly sold by dealers such as Baker. Still, Baker was anxious to meet Stanky, and I arranged a conference at the hospital—my second visit to the injured player that day. Baker and Stanky hit it off, and before long they were in agreement to do the program. In lieu of $500 per week, Stanky received a new car—made in England—called an Anglia. Since he only did the program for a month, it was a much better deal for him. The station received no money, and I received no talent fee, although I was the host and producer. But it did give badly needed recognition to WVOM and to me. Bill Sullivan, who later founded the Patriots, was the public relations director of the Braves. He was delighted with the broadcast. He saw to it that my picture was in the World Series program. New England was baseball-mad in 1948 as the Red Sox challenged Cleveland for the American League pennant, eventually losing out. The Braves, despite losing Stanky for a spell, went on to win the National League pennant, but lost the World Series title to Cleveland.

1949 NCAA Hockey Championship

Perhaps my most significant contribution to WVOM was to persuade the station to cover the 1949 NCAA hockey championship in Colorado. The NCAA hockey tournament had begun the previous year. Thayer Tutt, the owner and manager of the Broadmoor Hotel in Colorado Springs, had decided to sponsor it. With a hockey rink as part of the complex of the beautiful resort area in the foothills of the Rockies, Tutt had made his arena a home for the Colorado College hockey team, and a site for the NCAA hockey championship. Seating capacity was only 4,000, so revenue from the event was not going to pay for the cost. It was an attraction, though, and for Tutt it was a worthwhile promotion.

Four teams were in the 1949 tournament. Colorado College and Michigan represented the West, and Boston College and Dartmouth represented the East. As part of his arrangement for hosting the event, Tutt had to pay the expense of flying the teams to Colorado Springs and housing them for four days. At WVOM, we had broadcast many high school and college games throughout the season, and I was anxious to cover the tournament. I contacted Mr. Tutt, and he quickly approved free transportation aboard the charter flight, as well as free board and room at the hotel.

The engineering and line costs were $600. A total of $1,800 was needed for three games. The rosters of Boston College and Dartmouth were filled mostly by players from Greater Boston high schools. It was just as important to cover the Dartmouth-Michigan game as it was to broadcast Boston College and Colorado College.

Coca-Cola came on board for a third of the needed revenue, and Walter Brown, general manager of the Boston Garden, generously allotted $600 from his *Ice Follies* budget. Getting a third sponsor wasn't easy. People who had pre-war radios in 1949 simply could not get the station, so sponsors were scarce. For the final third, I turned to a Boston College alumnus, Ed Gallagher. His brother, John, was a solid defenseman on the Eagle team. Ed was a top executive in a prestigious insurance company, Kaler, Carney, and Liffler. During the broadcasts, the Coca-Cola and *Ice Follies* commercials were on recordings that were played on cue at the studio. Kaler, Carney, and Liffler left their commercials for me to do live.

It was a great series from a New England point of view. In the first game, Dartmouth upset the defending champions, Michigan, and in the second game, Boston College beat Colorado College. It set up an all-East battle for the title. It was a thrilling game, and the Eagles won 4–3. The Riley brothers from Medford were standouts for Dartmouth. Butch Songin, from Walpole, led Boston College. He was a sturdy defenseman who could have immediately gone into professional hockey had the National Hockey League in those days been receptive to American players. As it was, he turned to pro football, quarterbacking Hamilton to a Grey Cup victory in Canada, and later playing for the Boston Patriots.

The little station that could, WVOM, had an exclusive. Twenty-five hundred fans turned out at the airport the next day to salute the national champions. No one was more delighted than sponsor Ed Gallagher. "You made Kaler, Carney, and Liffler sound like they were the third line playing for Boston College," he said to me.

In the intervening 50 years, the players of the 1949 team kept their friendships alive by forming the Pikes Peak Club, named for the Rockies attraction. On their 50th anniversary, the team members were inducted as a group into the Boston College Hall of Fame.

The Navy PR Unit

After a couple of years of civilian life, I had received notice that I could be a member of the Naval Reserve and obtain credit toward retirement, even though I had not been with any reserve unit since my discharge. In the First Naval District there was a unit called Public Relations Company 1–1.

I joined with the knowledge that there would be no pay. Meetings to obtain points would be twice a month. Each meeting was worth a credit toward the 50 points needed each year. Others could be secured by going on active duty for two weeks each year, and by completing correspondence courses. If 20 or more years of service were completed, at age 60 you would be paid a pension based on rank. It was a good move. I've been receiving a pension as a retired Navy captain for over 25 years.

In the unit were Vin Maloney, top announcer for WNAC and the Yankee Network; Arch MacDonald, a newscaster for Channel 4; Bill Schofield, chief editorial writer for the *Boston Traveler;* Dick Lamere, a reporter for the *Traveler,* Ed McGrath, a reporter for *The Boston Globe*; John Galvin, a feature reporter for *The Boston Globe*; Tom Horgan, an editor with the Associated Press; Ranny Weeks, a movie and broadcasting star; and Dick O'Connell, general manager of the Boston Red Sox. There were many more who were public relations executives with various New England companies. In all, we had about 40 members. The unit was held together by Bill Hearn, who annually selected the officer who would be in command of the projects to be completed. I was selected to lead one year, and at the same time I was promoted to captain. I made my 50 points by doing two weeks of active duty (with pay) each year and completing correspondence courses.

The Pentagon

When the Korean conflict broke out, I had been with WVOM for three years. I had broadcast just about every sport imaginable, with an emphasis on hockey—which included high school, college, and the Boston Olympics. The Navy was expanding and a notice was sent to our unit that the Department of Defense was looking for experienced public relations officers. I volunteered and was accepted. It meant moving my young family—Martha was joined by Ted in 1950—to Washington, D.C., as my service was basically in the Pentagon. There was a huge buildup in the public relations office under Clayton Fritchey. I counted 250 employees of various military and civilian ranks.

I served as a correspondent and announcer on a 30-minute program, called *Time for Defense*, that was broadcast weekly on the Mutual Radio Network. I traveled around the country to military camps and did features on various aspects of the war effort.

The experience was invaluable to a broadcaster trying to hone the craft, but I knew my interest was in sports and my heart was in New England. So I worked on getting Barbara, Martha, and Ted back to Boston.

CHAPTER SIX

The Men Who Shaped the Bruins

Frank Ryan was the first voice of the Bruins. He began broadcasting on radio in 1925, during the first season of the team's existence. His play-by-play reports were on WBZ, which was operating in conjunction with the *Herald Traveler* newspaper. Ryan had been a reporter for the paper, but he saw an opportunity in the new medium. He then became the public relations director of the team, a position he held along with his radio job until 1952. He only broadcast the home games, but in later years he would do some road playoff games.

Basically, Ryan covered the team's road games by doing a 15-minute recreation on WBZ from 10:45 to 11 p.m. Through the Western Union ticker, he would get the essentials: penalties, goals, and highlight plays. For the rest of his report, he used his imagination. The 15-minute report was given sequentially, so that the final score was not announced until the end. Frank Ryan had built his career into a one-man corporation. He broadcast Bruins home games, did a nightly sports show on WAAB, was publicity director of the Bruins, was a city of Boston assessor, did public relations for both Harvard University and Suffolk Downs (a race track). When he retired, the comment was that six people got jobs.

The summer before I was to be separated from the Navy, I heard that Ryan was retiring. I contacted Walter Brown, the team president, and he assured me that I was the leading candidate for the job. He was working out the details with WHDH, and since he wanted all games covered, the expense was a serious consideration.

Brown wanted Jack Crawford, an outstanding former Bruins defenseman, to be the analyst. Each of us was to receive the princely sum of $60 per game. Train travel cost nothing (as long as I slept in the upper berth). Hotels and cab fare were reimbursed by the team, along with $12 a day for meal money. I later learned that Walter Brown was persuaded to contribute $15,000 to help defray the expenses of the broadcast. It was a terrible deal for the Bruins, and so I told Walter and accompanied him to a meeting with Bill McGrath, the station's general manager. The $15,000 was rescinded for the second year of the contract, but that meeting did not endear me to McGrath. There were opportunities for getting a talent fee on a station like WHDH. There were pre- and postgame reports on their Red Sox games, but I never had the opportunity to do them.

When I succeeded Ryan, Brown insisted that WHDH, which was then taking over the broadcast rights, do all the games, home and away. WHDH was proud of its new format, which featured a five-minute news report on the half hour. Bill McGrath, the station's general manager, insisted that the Bruins broadcasts could not begin until 8:35 p.m. By the time we went on the air, almost half the game was over. It was the best coverage the Bruins could get.

During the early years, when I was broadcasting the Bruins, three men helped to shape the team: Weston Adams Sr., Art Ross, and Walter Brown. Adams was the owner and the unofficial chief scout. Ross was the team's great coach and general manager in its early years. Brown was a brilliant entrepreneur who helped to create the Celtics, the Boston Olympics hockey team, and continue the tradition of the Boston Marathon. He also served for a time as the president of the Bruins. He was instrumental in the nationwide development of the *Ice Capades*.

Weston Adams

Weston Adams inherited the Bruins from his father. He brought a dedicated interest to the game. He had been a goaltender at Harvard, and that gave him more than a casual knowledge about the sport, but he let the wily Ross run the team while he concentrated on the business end.

What appealed to Adams most was scouting, discovering young talent in the bleak and frigid outposts of Canada. He thought he had a knack for it, and successful or not, he pursued the avocation into the Orr years. Many were the home games when Orr was in his glory that Box One, the Adams family viewing post at Boston Garden, did not have the president in attendance. He was off to Weyburn, or Estevan, Saskatchewan, or up to Niagara Falls, Ontario, to chat with Hap Emms—whom he later hired as general manager of a slumping team. On one visit to Estevan, accompanied by the Bruins' chief scout, Harold Cotton, Adams commented as he entered the rink on the notable brightness of the place. "A new paint job?" he inquired.

"That's not paint," said Cotton, "that's rime." The temperature outside was zero, and the walls were covered with condensation.

In 1962, I was hired by RKO General—a media conglomerate—to televise 25 Bruins and Rangers home games to an experimental Pay TV station in Hartford, Connecticut. It meant I had to give up the Bruins radio job on WHDH. I checked with Mr. Adams. He said it was OK, but he was concerned about who would do the radio. WHDH set up an opportunity for Mr. Adams and me to hear the recordings of about a dozen candidates. One of them was Jim Lang, who was announcing games for the Estevan Bruins, the club's junior hockey franchise. Weston had met him and heard his play-by-play on his scouting trips out west. Weston notified him of the opportunity. Listening to his tape, I noted that he was a dead ringer, in voice and inflection, for Foster Hewitt, Canada's legendary hockey announcer. What impressed Weston was his impartiality in describing games between Estevan and Weyburn, a neighboring city. The final choice to be my successor rested with Mr. Adams. He picked Lang.

It didn't work out. The Bruins were in the doldrums, and finding something positive to say about them was difficult, but Lang seemed to lean on the negative. "Pennington hasn't had a point in 12 games," was a typical comment. As for his impartiality in Saskatchewan, it turned out that Lang's father owned a good portion of both communities, including the radio stations, so his broadcasts were completely neutral. When the season ended, Adams had enough of Lang. Bob Wilson got the job and went on to a Hall of Fame career.

The Bruins have a theme song, thanks to Weston Adams. It's "Paree," a spirited tune that Weston enjoyed listening to when it was played by Jacques Renard and his orchestra at the rooftop nightclub at the Westminster Hotel in Boston.

There were no bands to play the song when the Bruins skated out to warm up, just John Kiley and a Hammond organ, perched in a couple of rows at the east end of the Garden. Mostly John played background music, and when the game was on, not being a fan, he stayed in the East Lobby, smoking a cigarette or two. The Bruins let the game speak for itself, unlike the Blackhawks, who had the mighty Wurlitzer reverberating in Chicago Stadium during the game.

Art Ross

C. F. Adams, the original owner of the Bruins, hired Art Ross in 1924 to be the team's general manager. Ross left his mark in many ways on the National Hockey League. His experience went back to the birth of the league. As a player, he was a superb competitor for 14 years. His talent got him selected to the Hall of Fame. But he was much more. He was a pioneer, innovator, strategist, promoter, coach, and general manager.

I knew him at the end of his career. He had turned over the reins as general manager of the Bruins to Lynn Patrick in 1953, yet he continued to come to the office and lend his advice. I had started as the Bruins broadcaster a year earlier and I was happy to get any advice that he could impart. Ross had a dry sense of humor, and one of his traits was to cut short his conversations with anybody who bored him. If such a person engaged him in conversation and Ross reached his breaking point, he would signal "time's up" by tugging on his lapel. Lynn would quickly wrap it up and the guest would leave.

Ross left his mark in many ways in the NHL. He improved the design of the puck and the goal net. In 1958, I was named the analyst of the CBS TV *Hockey Game of the Week*. After the first telecast, I went to the Bruins offices to get Ross' opinion on how the production came over. It was a black-and-white telecast with no replays, but it was a start. Ross quickly pointed out that since the telecast was not in color, the two blue lines and the red line at the center ice all came over to the viewer as black. He said that in order to distinguish the red line, we should make it a line in red and white checks. I passed the information on to CBS, and they relayed it to the National Hockey League. Since then, the centerline has been checked in all arenas, even though the games are now telecast in color, and even though the red line has become irrelevant. It was a typical observation of the astute Art Ross.

Throughout the early years of the National Hockey League, Ross was in sync with the Patrick brothers, Lester and Frank, about what was needed to improve the game. In 1935, he hired Frank to coach the Bruins. Frank had been a superb player. He was a forward-thinking coach who brought innovations to the game that made it more appealing to the general public. Seeing a player shoot the puck into the stands to get a face off and a breather for himself inspired Frank to come up with the two-minute delay-of-game penalty.

The Patricks created the two blue lines to open up the center area for passing. In the early years, the goaltender was required to stand on his feet to make a save. They changed that rule. They numbered the players' uniforms. They defined and credited assists, brought substitutions on the fly, and instituted the penalty shot. The Patricks created the playoff system for hockey that ultimately led to the National Hockey League having four of the six teams in the League qualify for the playoffs. For people who didn't like the game (including some of the press), the whole idea was thought to be ridiculous. There is no ridicule now, because all the other sports have adopted the Patricks' idea.

Frank Patrick brought that background to the Bruins as he moved his family to Commonwealth Avenue in Boston, Massachusetts, ready to assume his assignment. Despite his imposing résumé, Frank Patrick's two-year stint with the Bruins was not a success, and reluctantly Art Ross took over.

On one point, though, Ross was mistaken. As television developed, he predicted that it would have a negative effect on attendance at sporting events. He never envisioned that televising hockey games and other sporting events would enhance attendance. He thought that people would stay home and watch Milton Berle and other popular programs, and arenas like the Boston Garden would become empty. So he sold his stock in the team, figuring that the sport could never compete with this innovation.

It's hard to believe what a tough sell the Bruins were to broadcasters in those days. As noted, in 1958, I not only did the Bruins radio broadcasts, but I began a four-season career televising the National Hockey League *Game of the Week* on CBS TV. I was the analyst and Bud Palmer was the play-by-play man. The ratings weren't good around the country, but in Boston they were excellent. Going head-to-head with the NBA on NBC TV, hockey won by a three-to-one margin. Even though the games were on black-and-white TV with no replays, the fans followed the sport.

When the CBS series ended, I could not persuade anybody in the management of the Boston television stations to televise some Bruins games. They lived by the ratings, but in this case, they ignored them. In 1963, I noticed the Bruins schedule had three Saturday nights in a row where the team played in Toronto (twice) and Montreal. I tried to get any one of the four Boston TV stations (Channels 2, 4, 5, and 7) to give up half an hour on Sunday morning to televise the highlights of the Bruins' three Saturday night games. They could get a half-hour program with obvious local interest at no charge. They all refused.

I went to the Manchester, New Hampshire, station, WMUR-TV, and talked to Sam Phillips, the general manager. It wasn't an ideal situation, but at least the fans north of Boston would get to see the action. The only promotion was a couple of announcements on the public address system at the Garden. Channel 9 usually didn't go on the air until noon on Sundays, so Phillips had no problem in agreeing to an 11 a.m., one-hour show. Weston Adams Sr. agreed to pay *Hockey Night in Canada* $250 for each game—a total of $750. I taped the games in the CBC studios, drove all night to Concord, New Hampshire, slept for a few hours, then got to Manchester in time to broadcast each game by adding a voiceover to the edited tape.

I wanted to show the television executives and the advertising men that the Bruins, despite their lowly record, had a large fan base. There was no chance to get a Boston rating from a New Hampshire station. However, I made a few promotional announcements during the broadcasts. I made an offer of a Bruins calendar to those writing in. An incredible total of 2,500 cards and letters came streaming into the Bruins office. Many of them were letters, and basically they said, "Never mind the calendar, get the games on television." I took the boxes of mail to Ingalls Advertising. They handled the Volkswagen account. It was an immediate sale. They agreed to provide advertising for games that we could film or tape for the rest of the year. The next year, with a $25,000 rights fee going to the Bruins, the games wound up on Channel 5.

Then the arrival of Bobby Orr and a couple of independent television stations—Channels 56 and 38—changed the television picture in Boston. When TV38 finally landed the rights, Bobby Orr was at the top of his game. The ratings went through the roof.

Walter Brown

One of the people who always saw the value of pro hockey (and pro basketball) in Boston was Walter Brown. Brown is usually thought of today as the man who created the legendary Boston Celtics, but Walter was a hockey man to begin with. He took over the direction of the Boston Garden Arena Corporation in 1937, succeeding his father who had died. In 1936, he managed the U.S. Olympic hockey team when they played in Europe. When they returned, he kept many of them together (especially those who came from Greater Boston), and formed a team called "The Olympics." They played in the Quebec Senior League and on Sunday afternoons regularly drew a crowd of 16,000 fans to Boston Garden. At night, the Bruins drew another 16,000—32,000 hockey fans in one day.

Hockey was *the* sport in Boston in the '30s. In pro football, the Boston Redskins (now the Washington Redskins) drew only about 8,000 fans on average to Braves Field. In baseball, the Red Sox and Braves rarely sold out. Playing afternoon games, their fans would fill only half of Fenway Park and Braves Field. There was no professional basketball.

Brown had many interests. He was a primary investor in the *Ice Capades*, and much of the money he made from that choice arrangement helped to pay for his Celtics venture. The *Ice Capades* were a cross-country sensation, packing arenas with classic family-oriented shows. Brown obtained the best dates of the year for the Boston Garden, the Christmas season.

Walter also succeeded his father as manager of the now world-famous Boston Marathon. Of course, back then the Marathon had strictly amateur participants. The big money would come later. Brown held an annual Boston Athletic Association indoor track meet at the Garden to provide funds to keep the historic run operating.

But Walter could not do it without the help of Jock Semple, one of 20th-century sports' great characters. An ex-runner, Semple had set up shop as a trainer, and Brown found him space in the bowels of the Garden. Scottish-born Jock, who had never lost his accent, treated an array of brokers, bankers, lawyers, and others to what he called a rubdown—heavy accent on the "r." One customer termed it "hangover haven." His ministrations were frequently interrupted with calls about the marathon, and just as regularly, Jock, dressed in a T-shirt, white ducks, and sneakers, would walk into Walter Brown's office (the door seemed to be always open), and relay the latest information or complaint about the race. He would linger on and engage in a three-way conversation with Walter's guest. Jock brought informality to a new level. Will Cloney, a former sports writer and editor, was the director of the Boston Marathon, but Jock did the groundwork.

As a bonus for Jock, Walter arranged for him to be an unofficial trainer to the Boston Bruins when they were in the playoffs. He loved the hockey players for their gritty play, aversion to pain, and congenial attitude. So there would be no conflict with the team's regular trainers, Semple set up shop in his hotel room. In addition to physical comfort, he dispensed philosophical guidance on life's problems.

Players and management thought that Jock was a welcome addition at playoff time.

My association with Brown went beyond announcing duties. In 1964, I worked on his behalf to get new money into the Celtics. Walter had taken on ownership of the Celtics in a 50–50 deal with Lou Pieri, owner of the Providence Arena, when the Boston Garden Arena Corporation gave up on professional basketball in Boston. While Pieri owned half the team, he let Walter run it completely, and refused to invest any more money. It was a terrible arrangement for Brown. There was red ink all over the place. Only the skillful manipulations of Eddie Powers, the treasurer of the Celtics, the Garden, and the Bruins kept the Celtics afloat.

The money problems took their toll. Walter had a regular press luncheon on Mondays to talk about basketball at the Hotel Lenox. The publicist of the team, Howie McHugh, would distribute a press release and there would be speeches, maybe by a player, sometimes by a coach, but always a windup talk from Walter Brown. Annoyed by the lack of patronage, he would generally pour out his disgust at some problem or player. The result would be anything but positive public relations for the team. It was revealed later that Walter and the Celtics owed the Lenox for the luncheons for 10 years before finally settling. Walter lived the good life. He enjoyed a good martini or two and the fine food served by the exclusive Algonquin Club on Commonwealth Avenue in Boston. Membership in the Algonquin gave him access to occasional golf outings at the Oyster Harbors Club, one of Cape Cod's elegant venues. His attitude toward golf was indifferent, and his game showed it. I had the pleasure of accompanying him at both places as his guest. On the Cape, he had a substantial summer place in Centerville, just up the road from Craigville Beach. His wife,

Marjorie, was an avid beach person, but Walter could take the water or leave it. Swimming was not his thing, nor did he believe in any exercise. Our family would visit the Cape for a couple of weeks in the summer, and since we rented somewhat near Walter, I would ride with him to Boston a couple of days a week. Departure time was a leisurely 9 a.m. in Walter's Buick with "CELTIC 1" license plates. There was no hurry, so if Walter was going 50 miles per hour, he was speeding. He liked the recognition he got as the cars whizzed by, the drivers honking their horns and giving him a friendly wave. But each time a number of them had passed him, he would speculate that they were just fair-weather fans, and that obviously, from the low attendance at the Celtics games, they were not among his customers.

Walter constantly sought a more cooperative partner than Lou Pieri. I had known Walter Brown since 1947, having broadcast on radio for his Boston Olympics hockey team. Since I had gotten a television contract for the Bruins, a team that could not make the playoffs in 1964, he sent me to St. Louis to try to get Budweiser to sponsor some Celtic games on television. Walter advised me when I got to St. Louis to visit Ben Kerner, owner of the St. Louis NBA franchise. Kerner did not have a robust franchise. His main source of income was a Budweiser sponsorship. He did not want me to disturb his relationship, and I was careful not to. The company did put together a package on TV38, a struggling station at the time, but the effort did little to increase the Celtics' box office. Harry Caray, the St. Louis Cardinals baseball broadcaster, did the games. Interestingly enough, the Budweiser executives inquired into the possibility of sponsoring the Bruins games. I told them that the Bruins were all set. Their interest had been sparked by Jack McNamara, New England manager of Budweiser, who told them the area was hockey country.

Budweiser later became a huge sponsor when the games were on TV38, and they became beneficiaries of the Orr years.

As a broadcaster, I had connected with RKO General in 1962 when I was hired to televise 25 hockey games from New York and Boston on Channel 17, a pay TV station in Hartford, Connecticut. It was an experiment by RKO General that cost the company millions of dollars before they abandoned it.

I thought that Walter Brown and RKO General would be the perfect combination to operate the Celtics. I set up a meeting in August 1964 in New York between Brown and RKO General Vice President John Pinto. "How much for 50-percent ownership of the Boston Celtics?" Pinto asked. Walter didn't have a precise answer to Pinto's question, but ultimately he said, "About $2 million." There were further discussions about the team, the league, and Lou Pieri. Pinto said that he would get back to him after talking the proposition over with his general manager. At the time of these discussions, I was now Radio/TV director of the Bruins and Celtics. My salary was $150 per week. Each team paid $75.

Scarcely a week later, Walter Brown died at Cape Cod Hospital after a series of heart attacks. He was 58 years old. The sports world was stunned. Needless to say, I was called by Red Auerbach, Eddie Powers—who had succeeded Walter as head of the Boston Garden—and by Marjorie Brown and others about the New York talks. I had nothing to report. Apparently, John Pinto could not sell his general manager or the board of directors on the deal. My work for the Celtics ended with Brown's death.

Walter Brown's image has faded in the last 40 years. Only Boston University paid him tribute by naming their hockey arena after him. But when they built a new arena, they named it after Harry Agganis, a great athlete, but he never laced on a pair of skates. Brown was a sports pioneer. He was elected to the National Hockey League's Hall of Fame in 1962 after having served 13 years as president of the Bruins. The NBA's championship trophy is named after him. Given all of his contributions, especially to basketball, it is surprising that no book has been written or TV documentary made about him.

CHAPTER SEVEN

Hockey in the 1950s

When I began covering the Bruins at home and on the road in 1952, we traveled by train to the other five hockey towns: Montreal, Toronto, Detroit, Chicago, and New York. The Bruins had their own Pullman car with enough berths to handle the squad. There was a stateroom at one end for the coach, and a lounge at the other end that could handle seating for about eight people. I was assigned an upper berth, and in the two years that I traveled by train, never got a lower one. Sleep was a restless affair for me, while most of the well-conditioned athletes had no trouble with it.

The Montreal trip was overnight, with a locomotive change in White River Junction, Vermont, at about 4 in the morning that ensured everybody would be jarred awake. We stayed at an elegant Montreal hotel, the Chateau Champlain. After breakfast, I usually took a five-minute walk with Tom Fitzgerald of *The Boston Globe* up to the Sun Life Building. The National Hockey League headquarters were located there. Clarence Campbell, president of the National

Hockey League, always welcomed the visiting media and no appointment was necessary for an hour of hockey talk.

Later in my tenure, we flew to Montreal on a charter jet. After checking into the hotel, the routine was dinner at Moishes on St. Laurent Avenue. It was a steakhouse, and the steak was incomparable. Of all the restaurants on all of the trips, Moishes ranked number one with me. It was not a wide-ranging menu, and it was not a pretentious setting, but the food and service were top notch.

Montreal was hockey's mecca. A Saturday night game at the Forum was electric with excitement. In the early years of my coverage, two national anthems were sung by a superb tenor, Roger Doucette. The Canadian anthem was sung last, and as he reached the final lines, the capacity crowd would stand and give out an appreciative roar: "God keep our land glorious and free! O Canada, we stand on guard for thee! O Canada, we stand on guard for thee!" It had to be worth a goal a game for the Canadiens. It seemed as though energy just wafted out of the stands toward the Canadien players, not that the home team needed it. There was talent galore in their lineup. Rocket Richard, Doug Harvey, Tom Johnson, Jean Beliveau, Boom Boom Geoffrion, Dickie Moore, and later, Guy LaFleur. The games were hard fought, but the Canadiens usually won by a couple of goals.

After a Saturday night game, we boarded a train at Westmount station in Montreal, and the Montreal team car was attached. On most occasions, the train had to be held for the teams. Breakfast was somewhat awkward, with both teams using the same dining car. Imagine a Bruin enjoying a hearty breakfast when in walks a Montreal player, sporting a wound on his forehead inflicted by the Bruin player's high stick. Both players would know that the Sunday night game would be more intense. Backed by an enthusiastic, fired-up, sellout crowd at the noisy Garden, the Bruins would carry the play with a spirited attack that would feature hard-hitting body checks. Jacques Plante, in goal for Montreal, usually kept the game close. Whatever the outcome, the crowd was satisfied that they had seen hockey at its competitive best. Once, a snowstorm delayed the train and the teams barely made it to the Garden for the Sunday night game.

The Toronto trip was just a little longer; the arrival time was about 8 a.m. the next day. There was a short walk across the street to the old but elegant Royal York hotel. Detroit took even longer, and the early-morning arrival was accompanied by a trip to the worst, but the cheapest, hotel that the Bruins stayed in. It was the Leland, and the team rate was $5 a night per person. That was all it was worth. A Chicago trip meant a 3 p.m. departure and arrival the next morning. The hotel we stayed in was the LaSalle, and it wasn't much better than the Leland. There was no television in the room, and it cost a quarter for every 30 minutes that you wanted to listen to the radio. The visit to New York was a day trip and a stay at the Manhattan Hotel, which was just down the street from Madison Square Garden.

While there was discomfort in train travel for hockey teams, it meant the formation of a close-knit unit. They talked out their problems, successes, and disappointments. Postgame analysis went on long into the night following a game on the road. For me, it was a practical lesson in Hockey 101.

The travel during hockey season meant that I spent a quite of bit of time away from my growing family. My daughter, Sarah, was born in 1955, and Mary in 1958. Barbara, however, managed to keep everything running smoothly, and we were able to spend extra time together during the summers on Cape Cod.

The lack of sleep on the trains convinced me that I should fly, and I was the first to do so. Gradually, the Bruins shifted to air travel, and arrangements were made with commercial airlines. On occasions there were serious delays, but at no time did we miss a road game. Charter Airlines began to solicit the business of major league teams in all sports, and the Bruins joined in. Some of those charters proved to be highly unreliable, and sitting in a DC-3-type plane that was jammed to the doors with team equipment bags and the players was a perilous and claustrophobic experience. Gradually, the charters improved, and during the last three years of my service, the Bruins traveled in the most elegant jet imaginable. It left Hanscom Air Field with baggage stored below, had a tastefully designed interior with large leather seats, a well-stocked bar (not for the players), and conveyed nothing but the essence of luxury. When we landed, a bus was waiting on the tarmac to transport the team to its hotel. None of the inspection delays of commercial airlines were inflicted on the hockey team. It was a long way from the old Pullmans, and much appreciated.

At the beginning of my broadcasting career there were six teams, comprised entirely of Canadians. When I retired in 1997, the National Hockey League was comprised of 30 teams, some of them located in such ice-free areas as Florida and Southern California. The players were a polyglot crew who came not only from Canada and the United States, but also from Russia and Europe.

These hockey players made an impression on me.

Eddie Shore

There was no television to record his exceptional talent, but Eddie Shore's on-ice accomplishments—his sturdy body checking, his rink-length rushes, and his all-around physical style of play—made lasting impressions on Bruins fans. I saw him play in 1929 when I was 11. He dominated the game in a Bruins win. C.F. Adams, the Bruins owner, had paid the Edmonton Oilers $50,000 for Shore and six other players. The deal made the Bruins franchise, resulting in a Stanley Cup win in 1929. Shore won four Hart trophies as the League's most valuable player.

When I joined the team in 1952, Hammy Moore was the team trainer. He had been there during the Shore era. In the Pullman lounge, Hammy would entertain us with Shore stories. Hammy said of Shore, "He was the only player I ever saw who had the whole Garden standing every time he rushed down the ice. He would end up bashing somebody, get into a fight, or score a goal." His bashing of Ace Bailey, a Toronto forward in a game on December 12, 1933, resulted in Bailey being knocked unconscious and having to undergo emergency surgery to relieve pressure on the brain. Bailey recovered and led a normal life as an official at Toronto home games. Shore apologized, but the issue haunted him for the rest of his life.

Nearing retirement, Shore bought the Springfield Indians of the AHL while he was still playing for the Bruins, and split his season between the two clubs. He felt that by playing some games for the team he owned, he would help attendance. The Bruins didn't like the arrangement and traded him to the New York Americans, where he wound up his career. He became notorious as an eccentric owner who imposed strange rules of conduct on his players, coaches, and employees. He was known to make his players tap dance for an hour at a time. He maintained that it gave them balance. He fired two publicity directors because they refused to help him scrape the ice after a game. He asked players' wives to forego sexual activity before a game because it would diminish the productivity of his players. He made money with the team, and his frugality paid off, allowing him to promote hockey among children. He coached youth hockey teams and contributed money to support their programs.

Looking back over the years as a broadcaster of Bruins games, my deepest regret is that we never interviewed Shore on either radio or television. He was not far away, as the owner of the Springfield Indians, and his contribution to the Bruins in their early days was substantial. He was controversial, but that would have made for a more interesting interview. He did not attend Bruins games so we would have had to go to Springfield, but it would have been worth it.

The only time I met him was in 1982 at a game the Bruins were playing in Hartford. By that time, he had sold his interest in the Springfield team. He recognized me, and I initiated a conversation. We talked about Bobby Orr, and Eddie's comment was that he thought that Orr was a terrific player who would have been just as good in the six-team National Hockey League. I reminded him that Bobby's first year was in the six-team League, and he did not look out of place at all. Shore thought that Orr would have enjoyed the more intense rivalry of the League before expansion. He was enthusiastic about Terry O'Reilly and said, "He plays like I did." Shore didn't think much of the Hartford operation, although there was a sellout crowd there that night. It seemed at times as though the Bruins had as many fans there as the locals. I had to return to the broadcast booth, and so our chat was all too short.

Johnny Peirson

Peirson had two careers with the Boston Bruins. He spent ten years as a solid right winger, four times scoring 20 or more goals, and had 27 goals in the 1949–50 season. For most of his career, the team traveled by train, which gave him an opportunity for long conversations with the teammates and coaches. Hockey, of course, was the primary topic. When it came to a discussion of the strategy and tactics involved in the game, Peirson was prominent.

In the 1957-58 season, as the analyst and intermission interviewer for the CBS network hockey telecasts, I was anxious to talk to the most articulate players. At one Bruins game, I selected Peirson to do a feature on hockey sticks, their dimensions, rules about them, how players treated them, etc. He did a superb job. In 1969, WBZ took over the radio rights to the Bruins. I was named play-by-play man, and Jim Lightfoot, the station's general manager, asked me who could do the analysis. I recommended Peirson, and he got the job without an audition.

WBZ was and is a powerful radio station, heard in 38 states and Canada. With Bobby Orr reaching his peak, the team was becoming a powerhouse in the NHL. Peirson did a splendid job as analyst. His knowledge of the game, and how a team and individuals should play it, was a given. He prepared himself for each game and his vision was flawless. From time to time, I depended on his keen sight. After some goals, I could not be sure which player had scored. John would reach across and point out the number of the player who he thought had scored. I would go with that name, and it was invariably right. He did not voice his opinion, but rather gave the information to me.

In the spring of 1970, the Bruins won the Stanley Cup, with Bobby Orr scoring the winning goal against St. Louis. WBZ had a terrific season. The Bruins television station, WSBK-TV, Channel 38, had what might be termed a restless season. They had tried various analysts to work with play-by-play man Don Earle, but none could compare with Peirson's work on WBZ. The solution for Bill Flynn, the general manager of TV38, was to hire Peirson. Johnny came to visit me and said that while he had the offer and it was attractive, he was reluctant to take it, since he enjoyed working with me, and I had given him his start in the broadcasting business. I told him that while he would be tough to replace, he should take the job. It was a great opportunity. Peirson took the job, and Cal Gardner, a former Bruins player living in Toronto, became the radio analyst. He compiled a lot of frequent-flyer miles commuting to Boston for the home games, but WBZ paid the freight.

The 1970–71 season proved equally fabulous, as the team compiled 121 points, winning 57 of 78 games. They were known individually and collectively as "The Record Breakers." I made a recording at Fleetwood Records of the highlight season, but sales were disappointing after the club collapsed in the first round of the playoffs when the Canadiens upset them. Bill Flynn, at Channel 38, approached me after the season about joining Peirson as the play-by-play man. I was delighted, although somewhat reluctant to leave WBZ. Its powerful signal allowed people all over the country to hear me. Transplanted New Englanders were able to follow the fortunes of a team that was dominating hockey. I was the messenger, and the message was almost always good.

Peirson and I proved to be a good fit at Channel 38. My method was to call the play as accurately as possible, and then get out of the way for John's analysis. He saved Channel 38 quite a bit of money in one aspect of the telecast. On the road, they should have rented an additional camera for slow-motion replays of highlights, particularly goals. Instead, the station opted to do the replays back at the studio. That was fine as far as the viewing audience was concerned, but it meant that Peirson had no replay to look at. He was "flying blind." What he did was wait a few seconds after the goal was scored and then offer his interpretation of what happened leading up to the score. It turned out that his observations were accurate every time. As far as the viewer at home knew, Peirson was watching the replay with them. He brought his keen analysis to every facet of the game and was easily the best in the National Hockey League.

Milt Schmidt

He is the quintessential Bruin. His 16-year playing career is replete with All-Star selections, a Hart Trophy, Stanley Cups, and general leadership skills that epitomize the quality of the man. Schmidt, as general manager, made the trade that has been recognized as one of the greatest in National Hockey League history. Recognizing that sensational rookie Bobby Orr would need teammates to help him, Schmidt signed Phil Esposito, Fred Stanfield, and Ken Hodge from Chicago. In the trade, he gave up Pit Martin, a forward; Gilles Marotte, a defenseman; and Jack Norris, a goaltender. In a couple of years, this meant Stanley Cup time in Boston.

When I joined the team as a broadcaster, Schmidt was near the end of his playing career, but you could still see the fierce determination that was in his makeup. He had all the skills a play-making center needed, with an extra emphasis on the physical aspects of play. During the lounge conversations on the train, Schmidt's comments were always appreciated, and his stories of his confrontations with aggressive players like Black Jack Stewart, the Detroit defenseman, or Teeder Kennedy, the Toronto forward, were entertaining. On Christmas Day, 1954, he was named coach of the team. That meant he slept in the private compartment at one end of the train, and the long-time camaraderie he had with his teammates was cut back.

I remember once in New York, Schmidt was coaching a game in which the Bruins led the Rangers with one minute and 30 seconds left in regulation, by a score of 4–3. The Rangers had a player named Camille Henry, who was a devastating scorer, especially when he was on the power play. In his first year, he won the Calder Trophy scoring 24 goals. It was a time when players who scored just 20 goals were a rarity. The Bruins had two men in the penalty box, and the Rangers only one, giving New York a five-on-four advantage. There was a lot of open ice for Camille Henry to operate in. There was a face-off in the Ranger end, and Schmidt called a time out. During it, he spoke to Jerry Toppazzini, a decent player who gave the same spirited effort to each game that his coach did. Schmidt told "Topper" to take the face-off. He also told him to start a fight with Dave Creighton, a former Bruin (now a centerman for New York), before the face-off. The aim of the fisticuffs was to engage Creighton sufficiently to draw a penalty on him. Done properly, both men would go to the penalty box, but of course Toppazzini's would be delayed, since the Bruins already had two men in the box. Jerry, not known for his fighting ability, put on a superb act and drew a startled Creighton into a grappling match that netted each of them two-minute penalties. The teams went on to play four against four. The Bruins were able to stymie Henry, and held on for a 4–3 win.

As a coach, Schmidt was one of five people who got credit for discovering Bobby Orr. He was in Ganonoque, Ontario, to help evaluate two other Bruins prospects when the 12-year-old caught the quintet's admiration. Having played with the legendary Eddie Shore and been a partial discoverer of Bobby Orr, Milt Schmidt's career spans the years in the franchise's greatest history.

Fernie Flaman

A Hall of Famer since 1990 and deservedly so, Fernie came to Boston as a 16-year-old. The Bruins assigned him to the Boston Olympics of the Eastern Hockey League as the infusion of local Greater Boston players diminished and more Canadian players were in the lineup. From the outset, Fernie was a fan favorite. He was a hard-hitting defenseman who could deliver open-ice body checks and keep the front of the net clear. He was an Eastern League all star for two of the three years he played with the Olympics. In 1947 he joined the Bruins and played for five years before he was traded to Toronto, joining the Stanley Cup team in 1951. He later rejoined the Bruins and played seven years with the team. After retirement, he served in the minor leagues before being named head coach of Northeastern University. He served in that capacity for 19 years. He was named U.S. Coach of the Year in 1982 and won the Hockey East Championship in 1989.

Mr. Zero

When you think about it, it's not exactly a wonderful nickname to have—"Mr. Zero." But that's what they pinned on Frank Brimsek shortly after he joined the Bruins in 1938. Brimsek was a two-time All-Star and a member of the National Hockey League's Hall of Fame. "Mr. Zero" as a moniker doesn't rank up there with "Rocket" Richard, or "The Edmonton Express," as Eddie Shore was called. If you were a banker or a carpenter, and they called you "Mr. Zero," it would not be taken as a compliment. Despite all of that, it fit Frank Brimsek well.

Brimsek was playing with the Providence Bruins Cubs of the American Hockey League when Art Ross, the Bruins' general manager, brought him up. It was a pressure-cooker situation. Tiny Thompson had been the Bruins goaltender since the 1928–29 season (a Stanley Cup year). He was one of the most popular players on the team. However, he had had contract disputes with Ross, and early in the 1938–39 season, Ross decided to do something about it. The GM was taking a big gamble, but he very much liked Brimsek's work in Providence.

The Bruins started the season with an impressive record of five wins, one loss, and one tie. Thompson was the goaltender. On November 29, 1938, Thompson was sold to the Detroit Red Wings. Brimsek, ten years younger, and with a salary nowhere near Thompson's, made his debut against the Montreal Canadiens on December 1. The Bruins lost 2–0, and back in Boston, Ross and Brimsek were roasted. The Bruins won their next three games, and they were all shutouts for Brimsek. His fifth game was a 3–2 victory over Montreal. He then turned in three more shutout wins. In seven games, the young goaltender had allowed only two goals. The fans went wild, and the sobriquet "Mr. Zero" was born. Art Ross was hailed as a genius, and Tiny Thompson was soon forgotten.

With Brimsek in the nets, the team finished with a 31–9–1 record, the class of the League. In the playoffs, the Bruins and their rookie goaltender were up against a talented New York Ranger team. The series went to a seventh game. Tied at 1–1 in regulation, the clubs went to midway in a third overtime before Mel Hill scored for a Boston win. It was the third game of the grueling series to go to overtime, and in each of them Hill scored the winner. Forever after, Hill was known as "Sudden Death" Hill. There must be a wrestler who has adopted the name since. In the seven-game series, Brimsek had allowed only 12 goals. With so many games stretched into overtime, the teams had played the equivalent of nine games. The rookie in goal had never buckled under pressure.

The next series, against Toronto, for the championship and the Bruins' second Stanley Cup, was a comparative breeze. The Bruins won in five games. Brimsek allowed only six goals. Brimsek won the Vezina Trophy for allowing the fewest number of goals in a season. He was also the winner of the Calder Trophy as Rookie of the Year. Two years later, Brimsek guided the Bruins to another Stanley Cup win. In the finals against Detroit, he only allowed six goals in four games.

The late Woody Dumart, the stellar left wing on one of the Bruins' best lines ever in their 75-year history—the Kraut Line— remembered Brimsek well. Dumart had been in touch, even though Brimsek had not joined in many Bruins alumni get-togethers.

"He was a superb goaltender," Dumart recalled. "He was a stand-up type, as were most of those early goaltenders. He had the quickest glove hand of any goaltender I have ever seen play. I tested him a lot in practice, but he was hard to beat. Occasionally, I would inadvertently fire a high shot at him. It was long before goaltenders wore masks, and he resented that more than anything. The next time I came in, I would find that Brimmie had left the net. Got the word— keep your shots low. He had a great knack of giving you an opening, and when you went for it, he would take it away with a flashy glove maneuver."

Brimsek had a reserved personality. He prepared for a game unobtrusively. The Bruins had an All-Star defenseman, Jack Crawford, who was just the opposite. Ebullient and outgoing, Jack was a chatterbox before a game. On occasion he would try to talk it up with Brimsek. "How do you feel, Frank?" he would ask. "Lousy," Brimsek would reply. "Great," Crawford would respond, "we'll win the game."

After wartime service, Brimsek returned to the Bruins, but his talent had lessened somewhat. Brimsek retired in 1950 after playing a total of 70 games with the Chicago Blackhawks. His last year with the Bruins was 1949. Back in his hometown of Eveleth, Minnesota, he became a railroad engineer. For the most part, he stayed at home and never joined teammates and opponents in any kind of reunion. As a member of the Hockey Hall of Fame, he could have attended the annual induction ceremonies as a guest. He never did. "Mr. Zero" was content to let his record speak for itself.

Cliff Thompson

Thompson was an All-Star defenseman at Stoneham High School in the Greater Boston Interscholastic Hockey League, and by 1940 was playing defense for the Boston Olympics. In 1941, at age 22, he played six games with the Boston Bruins. Although brief, his appearance was a major accomplishment, because American-born players were still not well received in the NHL at that time.

After the war, Thompson played ten games with the Bruins in 1948, but most of his work was with the Boston Olympics. By 1955, he was a linesman in the NHL, and on the fateful night of March 15 was working the Boston-Montreal game. The legendary Rocket Richard of the Canadiens became embroiled with Hal Laycoe, a journeyman defenseman of the Bruins. Laycoe high-sticked him, and when Richard discovered blood from the blow, he went berserk and clubbed Laycoe. Thompson intervened, and took Richard's stick away as Laycoe dropped his. Richard got another stick and whacked Laycoe again. Thompson pulled him away, and for the third time, Richard got another stick and belted the defenseman. Thompson wrestled Richard away and had him tied up when another Montreal player came to Richard's aid. He threw a couple of haymakers at Thompson.

I tried to describe the action as best I could on radio. It was a scene worthy of the World Wrestling Federation. Later, Clarence Campbell, the president of the NHL, met with the participants, and suspended Richard for the rest of the season. Many of the French Canadians in Quebec thought it was an unfair decision. Campbell made his ruling because Richard struck Thompson. It was the second time that season that Richard had struck an official. Campbell, a Rhodes scholar and lawyer, was a former referee in the National Hockey League. He believed that officials had to be protected.

On March 17, Campbell attended a game between Montreal and Detroit at the Forum, and was taunted, assaulted, and mistreated by the fans. A smoke bomb was thrown, and the building had to be evacuated. Campbell was lucky to escape as the fans continued down

St. Catherine's Street and rioted for seven hours. The crux of the situation was Richard hitting Thompson. Richard contended that he didn't know what he was doing because of the blow he received in the head. He said that hitting Thompson was an accident. He said he thought he was one of the Bruins, some of whom had been milling about. The whole episode was a harrowing experience for Cliff Thompson. And his reward? He never worked another National Hockey League game.

Hal Laycoe

There will be no recap of flashy goals scored, no rerun of memorable plays, no retired number lifted to the rafters when Hal Laycoe's name comes up as part of Bruins history. Just one night will be recalled—March 15, 1955, when Laycoe high-sticked Rocket Richard of Montreal. Laycoe was a unique individual. I knew him well both before and after the incident. His first year with the Bruins, Laycoe spent the off-season building a house in the exclusive town of Weston. Location meant everything to him, and in selecting Weston he picked the best. For the construction he was the "clerk of the works." He hired the architect, the masons, the carpenters, the plumbers, and presided over the whole operation. When finished, the house had to be worth $400,000. Now it would be worth several million dollars. Laycoe's salary hardly justified the cost, but he made it pay off with careful supervision.

Barbara and I lived in Newton just outside of Boston at the time, and our house was often a stopover for Laycoe and his wife after Bruins home games. He was a keen student of the game, and since he spent so much time on the bench, he was able to analyze and critique the play. It was more hockey than I wanted to absorb, but it was a learning experience.

To support that expensive house, Laycoe needed off-season work. In his second year with the team he became a car salesman for a Chrysler, Plymouth, and Dodge dealer. Before the next summer, he spoke to me about doing a sports show on radio. He knew that in 1948, I had lined one up for Ed Stanky of the Braves. The only difference between the two was that Stanky had a substantial reputation and was a key player, while Laycoe was simply the fifth or sixth defenseman in the Bruins scheme of things. I told Laycoe he would have to get a sponsor if he wanted to be on air. He soon lined up the Dodge dealers, and just as quickly he was on the air on WCOP. He had a good voice, was articulate, and did not have too much of a Canadian accent.

I knew where he was headed upon his retirement. He became a coach at New Westminster of the Western Hockey League, and continued in that capacity when the team became the Portland Buckaroos. He served as coach and general manager of the team for nine years. In seven of the nine years, they won the championship. They never had a losing season. In 1970 he took over as coach of the Vancouver Canucks of the NHL. Expansion teams struggle, and although he later became the general manager, the experience was a trying one. At the end of his hockey career, he began scouting for the New York Islanders. He was a man of talent, and his coaching record speaks for itself.

Jack Crawford

He was a major league hockey player, a coach, a broadcaster, and a successful businessman. Veteran Rhode Island hockey fans remember Jack Crawford as a coach who brought his Providence Reds team to a Calder Cup triumph in 1956. My memory of him is of a sturdy, stay-at-home defenseman with the Boston Bruins for 13 years. Most fans (and rivals) remember the shattering body checks he dealt. Others recall that he wore a helmet—one of the first NHL players to do so. He wore it for cosmetic reasons, having lost his hair as a young man. In no way did it resemble today's compulsory protection devices. In two of the seasons he played with the Boston Bruins, they won the Stanley Cup. In 1946, he was named to the NHL first All-Star team.

In Crawford's time in the majors, it was customary for the players to find summer employment to supplement their income. Milt Schmidt was a golf pro, Woody Dumart sold hockey equipment. Crawford moved to Cape Cod, and founded a paper product distribution business with his brother. He was always popular with his teammates and well liked by management, so after his retirement, he was offered the coaching job at Hershey, the Bruins' top affiliate in the American Hockey League.

In 1952, the Bruins were making a change in the broadcast booth. Their first and only play-by-play man, Frank Ryan, was retiring. I won the coveted job. For the first time, they were broadcasting away as well as home games on radio, so Walter Brown, then the president of the team, wanted to add a color man.

Jack Crawford was a logical choice for the position. With his business just beginning to flourish, he could live on the Cape and devote more time to it in the winter months. He became the first ex-player in the NHL to become a hockey analyst, and one of the first to do so in any sport. So it was Crawford and Cusick as the Bruins voices. I knew the game of hockey, and at that point had done many high school and college games, but Crawford knew the game from ice-level, and everybody from executives to players, to trainers, to stick-boys knew Jack Crawford. Walter Brown could not have made a better choice.

Crawford served as analyst for two years, and then opted to return to coaching. He wanted to be closer to the action, and since the offer came from Providence, he would still be near his Cape Cod home and his business. In the 1955–56 season, Crawford led the Providence Reds to a Calder Cup championship. It was to be the last time that Providence reached that pinnacle until rookie coach Peter Laviolette did it in 1998–99. Crawford had three All-Stars on the club. Zellio Toppazzini was a talented scorer, but could not do it when he had his chance in the NHL. Camille Henry could score in any league, and kept it up when he joined the New York Rangers. The stalwart of the team was Johnnie Bower, the goaltender. Seemingly destined for a career as a minor league goaltender, Bower later got a bid from Punch Imlach in Toronto. He backstopped the Leafs to Stanley Cup victories although he was well into his 30s, and the team in front of him was composed mainly of veterans.

Crawford later coached in Rochester and Baltimore before retiring in 1966. He returned to the sport when the Cape Cod Cubs were formed. He served as general manager. Jack passed away in 1973. There's no question that had expansion come earlier than 1967 in the National Hockey League, Jack Crawford would have been a coach in the majors. The opportunity never came, but in Providence, old-timers remember his contribution to a notable Calder Cup triumph.

Real Chevrefils

Hap Emms, who for a brief stretch was the Bruins' general manager, and who developed some outstanding junior hockey teams at Barrie and Niagra Falls, called Real Chevrefils the best hockey player he ever coached. A compactly built left winger with huge hands that enabled him to fire the puck with great accuracy, he was destined for All-Star honors and the Hall of Fame. Chevrefils was a winger on the Memorial Cup championship Barrie Flyers team. He was the property of the Boston Bruins, and was soon in their lineup. In the 1952–53 season, he scored 19 goals and was a key player in the Stanley Cup finals. But "Chevy" self-destructed. When I think of his brief career, I am leery of the liquor advertising that I see on hockey telecasts and other sports. Beer has long been an accepted sponsor, but in recent years hard liquor has been promoted. It does not send a good message to the youngsters just taking up the game of hockey and watching the telecasts. If they knew the Chevrefils story, they would be forewarned. Initially he was a beer drinker, but early in his career he started drinking hard liquor.

To the consternation of general manager Lynn Patrick, Chevrefils picked the playoffs to do his hardest drinking. In the 1956–57 season he hit the heights as—drinking or not—he scored 31 goals. Once again, the Bruins reached the finals against their archenemy, the Montreal Canadiens. The pressure was too much for Chevrefils. Patrick was so distraught that he had "Chevy" move into his house in Wellesley so he could keep an eye on him. It did no good, as

Chevrefils was obviously off the wagon when he faced Montreal. There is a classic picture of him on the cover of a sports magazine, a glazed look on his face and his skate laces untied. He was an alcoholic, and the Bruins could do nothing about it. By age 26 he was out of the National Hockey League for good, a sad ending to what looked like a very promising career.

Second Jobs

When I started with the team in 1952, the pay for players was so low that most had to get regular jobs in the off-season to help pay the bills. The players on the teams in the rest of the league were in the same predicament.

Woody Dumart was the Bruins' high-scoring left winger on the "Kraut" line, and to earn additional income he represented the Bauer Skate Company in New England. It was a company owned by the family of his linemate, Bobby Bauer, and turned out a quality product. His business expanded after retirement and he had a full-time position.

John Peirson entered his father-in-law's furniture business and studied it, from manufacturing through sales. It brought in summertime income and he had a 50-year career as a salesman after leaving hockey.

Bill Quackenbush attended Northeastern University and earned an engineering degree. After retiring from hockey, he secured the hockey and golf head coaching jobs at Princeton University.

Hal Laycoe had a brief radio career doing a nightly sportscast on WCOP, Boston, for one summer season.

Hap Emms, a former player, was owner/general manager of the Barrie Flyers, a championship junior hockey team. He later became general manager of the Bruins. In Barrie, he also owned an electrical business and employed some of his players. One was Leo LaBine, a fiery right winger, who played several years with the Bruins. One summer, Leo served as an apprentice electrician for Emms. It turned out to be a losing deal, however. Leo and his fellow workers managed to wire the wrong house. The tight-fisted Emms made them pay for it the rest of the summer. It was a costly job for Leo.

Ed Sandford went directly to the Bruins from junior hockey, and after a full season of professional hockey, went into construction work. It was outdoors, and it was heavy lifting. Sandford said that he enjoyed it so much that he did it for three summers before trying his hand as a car salesman.

Ferny Flaman and Pat Egan, a couple of rugged defensemen, were able to handle the physical aspects of truck driving. Flaman worked for Budweiser, and Egan for 7-Up. Both of them later wound up as hockey coaches, Flaman at Northeastern University and Egan with the Springfield Indians.

Milt Schmidt had a brilliant career with the Bruins as player, coach, and general manager. He recalls that his playing days were marred by bitter contract disputes with general manager Art Ross. Schmidt and the team prospered. After they won the Stanley Cup in 1941, Schmidt remembers that he and his linemates—Dumart and Bauer—went on strike until a $500 raise for each of them broke the deadlock. For off-season employment, Schmidt connected with George Page, who owned the Colonial Country Club in Lynnfield. Page was a tremendous Bruins fan and was delighted to have Schmidt's name associated with his operation. Milt was not a golf professional, but assisted where he could to make the course a popular place.

I was looking for added income myself, and started a hockey school. I promoted it on the radio broadcasts, lined up a hockey rink in Lynn, and hired a couple of Bruins as faculty members. We had about 25 students. I never entered that field again, even though it has proven very popular for many people who began hockey camps during the Orr years.

Fred Cusick
VOICE OF THE BRUINS

RIGHT: The future sportscaster at age six, with my family.

LEFT: The college graduate, 1942.

RIGHT: Northeastern University's first line, 1941. Left to right: me; John Chipman, center; and Eddie Barry, left wing.

Newly commissioned—
ready for sea.

With brother John, aboard the
SS William Asa Carter at
Barry, Wales, June 1945.

LEFT: Hard-hitting defensemen Jack Crawford—my first broadcast partner.

Photo by Steve Babineau/Sports Action Photography

BELOW: The Cusick family at Bruins Christmas party, 1953. Left to right: Barbara, Martha, Teddy, and me.

LEFT: Turning over command of Public Relations Company 1-1 to Lt. Cdr. Vin Maloney, who receives congratulations from Rear Admiral John Snackenberg.

ABOVE: Weston Adams (right) offers me congratulations on being picked to broadcast games on WBZ. The station's general manager Jim Lightfoot looks on.

LEFT: High scoring right winger John Peirson—later my broadcast partner. Photo by Steve Babineau/Sports Action Photography

ABOVE: The Boston Garden—my "office" for over 40 years.

Photo by Steve Babineau/Sports Action Photography

RIGHT: A promotional piece with John Peirson.

Our Cup wonneth over.

The Bruins on TV 38.

Brought to you by a winning team of sportscasters, Fred Cusick and Johnny Peirson.

In a switch Ray Bourque is interviewing me.

On the links with Bobby Orr, the greatest hockey player of all time.

With Clive Fazioli, ready to televise another *Tucker Anthony Golf Classic*.

Receiving the Lester Patrick Award from the NHL in 1988 for outstanding service to hockey in the United States.

LEFT: With Brad Park, ready to broadcast a Lowell Lock Monsters game.

RIGHT: Barbara and I celebrate our 50th wedding anniversary.

LEFT: Ready for a round of golf with Milt Schmidt.

CHAPTER EIGHT

Hockey—More than the Players

I n all my broadcasting career, the two seasons (1969 through 1971) I spent doing Bruins games on WBZ radio with Johnny Peirson had to be the most enjoyable. The 50,000-watt clear channel signal was heard in 38 states and Canada. There were a lot of transplanted New Englanders who followed the team regularly. They wrote long homesick letters to me about their Bruins.

The first year Boston won the Stanley Cup, and the second year they set all kinds of records stomping through the league, but they were stunningly upset in the first round of the playoffs. The Bruins suffered a bad case of overconfidence—bordering on cockiness— throughout the series, and when Bobby Orr came up with a groin injury for the deciding game, they were unable to deliver.

With the season shortened, I received a call from Bill Flynn, the general manager of TV 38. We met for lunch at the Pillar House in Newton. He wanted to know if I was interested in doing the Bruins television play-by-play. He had hired John Peirson away from WBZ the year before to be the analyst, but now he wanted me to take over the anchor position. I was amenable. When it came to money, I told him I wanted a year-round salary, and if that meant working full time I was agreeable. Essentially we settled on my joining the staff of the station with talent fees added once the season began. As a staff member, I would be available for announcing, interviewing, and promotional work. Best of all, I would be a part of the employee's health plan and pension system. Not many play-by-play sportscasters had a setup like that.   Most were freelance performers. I had security—or so I thought.

Foster Hewitt

In 1972, I also broadcast the Russia-Team Canada Summit Series. There was tremendous interest in Canada, and a modest amount in the United States. Bill Flynn obtained the American rights to the telecasts, and selected John Peirson and me to do the first four games, which would be played in Canada. Peirson took a special course at Berlitz to study the correct Russian pronunciations. I also did some massive preparation in order to be ready for the big event. We went to Montreal early to get a line on the two squads.

As part of our homework, we looked up Foster Hewitt to gain further insights. Foster was to handle the play-by-play for Canada, and just about the whole country would be watching. Hewitt was the pioneer of sports broadcasting, having begun hockey coverage in 1923, and staking his claim to fame with his play-by-play of the Toronto Maple Leafs. His Saturday night radio broadcasts, and, beginning in 1952, telecasts, made *Hockey Night in Canada* one of the nation's all-time favorites. Many people in the United States also heard and watched him.

Hewitt had done many international events, and was familiar with the Russian players. We had our Berlitz pronunciations and checked them over with him. How about Ragulin? We called him Ra-GOO-lin. "Oh, that's Rags, RAG-yew-lin," said Hewitt giving it his Anglicized pronunciation. "I've been covering him for years."

Hewitt had his own interpretation, and his word was law in Canada. We abandoned our quest for further information. He went on to cover all eight games.

Hewitt was the Grand Old Man of Canadian hockey announcers. When he began with the Leafs, the general manager, Conn Smythe, asked him where he would like to locate his announcing booth in the arena. Hewitt went to a local department store, climbed up five flights, and determined it was the perfect location—high enough to see all the action, yet close enough to identify players on the ice. That was the height he wanted at Maple Leaf Gardens, and the broadcasting gondola was built hanging from the rafters. Hewitt was alone at one end doing his broadcast. At the other end, visiting radio (and later television) was allowed. I occupied that visitor's spot for many years.

Before a game, the host team generally provided a meal—of varying degrees of quality. The press not only ate but also exchanged information about the teams. In all the years I covered Bruins games in Toronto, I never saw Foster Hewitt at any of those gatherings. When I arrived in the gondola, he would exchange pleasantries, but that was all. In 1957, after five years of doing television of the games, he turned the play-by-play over to his son, Bill. Foster concentrated on a radio station that he had built, CKFH. One of its features was the road games of the Maple Leafs.

When Hewitt came to Boston, there was no mingling with the media, neither press nor broadcast types. On one occasion though, he asked me for a favor. It seems that he had competition from a rival Toronto radio station. They were recreating Maple Leaf road games almost simultaneously with the action, and doing it so well that it sounded as though the broadcast was coming from Boston Garden. They had hired an engineer in Waltham, Massachusetts. He was redirecting my broadcast from his house and feeding it via the telephone to Toronto. The announcer there, while listening to me, was simply relaying it over the station's Toronto airwaves with recorded background noise. To prove this was being done, Hewitt asked me to change the time of a penalty. Instead of announcing that it was called at 8:36 for instance, I was to say that it was 8:37. I was to do this a couple of times. I did, and it helped Foster in his court case against the station. Hewitt soon had road broadcasts to himself.

Lynn Patrick

I'm not for the "what-if" category as in, "What if Bobby Orr didn't have all those knee problems and wound up with a 20-year National Hockey League career like Red Kelly?" Or, "What if the World Hockey League never existed to disrupt things in the NHL?" But there is one that I think about, and it concerns George "Punch" Imlach. That's not a very impressive nickname. He earned it in his playing days, when he received a concussion and acted strangely, causing a newspaperman to call him "punch drunk," which led to him being called Punchy and ultimately, Punch. The nickname belies Imlach's talent as a coach and general manager in the National Hockey League, where in 11 years of handling those two jobs with the Toronto Maple Leafs, he won four Stanley Cups and reached the finals two other times. At the same time, the Bruins were not even making the playoffs.

But Boston had first crack at his services when Lynn Patrick, the Bruins' general manager in 1957, offered Imlach the opportunity of being coach and general manager of the Springfield Indians of the American Hockey League. At the time, they were a farm team of the Bruins, although the irascible Eddie Shore owned the team and some of the players. For 10 years prior to the offer from Patrick, Imlach had directed the fortunes of the Quebec Aces, a senior amateur team in Quebec City. He was ready to move up, and Patrick had spotted his talent. Imlach had an unhappy year in Springfield, as he had to contend with the constant interruptions of Shore. I first met Imlach during that period, when he often came to Bruins games, and I had him as a guest between periods. At the time, WHDH had assigned John Day, the station's program director, to the games to handle commercials. John later became a well-known TV newscaster on Channel 4, but he was the first to admit he knew nothing about hockey. So I handled the intermission interviews as well as the play-by-play. It was obvious in these sessions with Imlach that he knew the game, and was headed for bigger things. He had a fine voice, was very articulate, and could have made a career as a radio or TV analyst.

He took the Springfield Indians to the finals in the American Hockey League, and Lynn Patrick was quick to acknowledge the feat. He offered Imlach the job of being farm director for Boston and a sort of troubleshooter for the organization. What if Imlach had agreed to that offer? Instead, he went to the League meetings, met with the Toronto executives, and mulled over an offer that was similar to what the Bruins presented. The Leafs had to get permission from the Bruins to negotiate with Imlach. In the course of weighing the two opportunities, Lynn Patrick became ill. He was sick enough to have Walter Brown, the team president, call Stafford Smythe, Toronto's owner, and tell him that the Bruins were changing their mind and not allowing Imlach the freedom to negotiate with another team. Smythe said that they were too far along in their talks. Punch decided that Toronto was the best opportunity, and that's where he went. His 11 years in those dual roles were not exactly smooth ones as the "Toronto Executive Committee" led by Smythe, constantly second-guessed him. Not while he was winning the Stanley Cups in 1962, '63, '64, and '67, but at other times. As he tells it in his biography, written with Scott Young, *Hockey is a Battle*, published by Crown Publishers Inc., he did it his way.

The coach of Toronto was Billy Reay, and shortly after the season began, Imlach fired him and took over both roles, as coach and general manager. He went with veterans in his lineup, drafting 34-year-old goaltender Johnny Bower out of Cleveland as a starter. None of them proved more valuable than Red Kelly, whom he acquired from Detroit. Kelly had been a brilliant defenseman for the Red Wings; an All-Star for eight consecutive years as the Wings won three Stanley Cups. For some reason, he was in disfavor with Detroit, and they traded him to the New York Rangers for Eddie Shack in 1960. He was 33 years old and decided to retire. Imlach, in Toronto, talked him out of it, and made a deal with Detroit by sending Marc Reaume there. But he didn't use Kelly on defense. Instead, he made him a center. Only a brilliant tactician like Imlach would make a move like that.

Several times, players who were excellent forwards finished their careers as defensemen. The best illustration of this move was the Bruins' captain, Dit Clapper, a top-performing right winger, who wound up his 20-year career on the blue line. Kelly played eight years as a forward for Imlach, and four of them resulted in Stanley Cup victories. Two other veterans from Detroit's highly successful teams of the '50s—defenseman Marcel Pronovost and Goaltender Terry Sawchuck—joined Kelly as the Leafs marched to a Stanley Cup win in 1967. Imlach was not without controversy. He worked his players hard, and some of them revolted. Frank Mahovlich and Andy Bathgate were two of the better ones who didn't like Imlach's hard-driving ways. But results are what count, and the general manager/coach could produce. What if the Bruins had had him, beginning in 1958?

As the Bruins' general manager, Lynn Patrick was always on the lookout for talented players. But, as in the Imlach case, he kept his eye out for astute managers and coaches. On a break in 1961 from the National Hockey League schedule, he was surveying a Bruins farm team in Kingston, Ontario. Harry Sinden was a player/coach. Patrick was impressed with his knowledge of the game, and his manner in handling and motivating the players. The next year he advanced Sinden to Minneapolis, and then to Oklahoma City. By 1966, Harry had guided that team to the Central Hockey League championship and he was named the coach of the Bruins.

By 1970, the Bruins had won the Stanley Cup. Sinden got in a salary dispute with management after the victory, and left the team for private enterprise. He was based in Rochester, New York, and told me that he followed the team regularly via the clear channel signal of WBZ radio. I was doing the games. He was given a chance to return to hockey in 1972 as coach of Team Canada in the Summit series against Russia. With John Peirson, I covered the first four games on an impromptu television network anchored by WSBK-TV 38 in Boston. Harry had a talented group of players, but the big question would be what kind of condition would they be in with the first game to be played on September 2? Peirson and I watched the Russians practice on September 1 in Montreal, and little did we realize that their indifferent and casual attitude was just a put on.

All of Canada was agog over the series, and most predicted a Canadian sweep of the eight games. Their chauvinism received a severe jolt with the first game. The well-conditioned Russians dominated in every phase and won 7–3. Sinden and his team of All-Stars were blasted by the press, reviled by the fans, and critiqued by the nation. Clarence Campbell, the president of the National Hockey League, led the way. In the best coaching performance that I have ever witnessed, Sinden was able to turn the tide with a 4–1 victory in Game 2, played in Toronto. The coach shook up his roster, adding toughness to the lineup with Wayne Cashman, J. P. Parise and Stan Mikita up front; and on defense he inserted Serge Savard, Bill White, and Pat Stapleton. Game 3 was a 4–4 tie, and Game 4 in Vancouver went to the Russians 5–3. Our broadcast assignment ended with that game, and the squads headed for Russia. In one of the great sports upsets of all time, Team Canada, led by Harry Sinden, was able to edge out the Russians with a dramatic goal by Paul Henderson in Game 8, for a 6–5 win. For Sinden, it was the series triumph of a lifetime, and he returned to the Bruins.

For Lynn Patrick, there was not much success as general manager of the Bruins, but he gets credit for the great career of another general manager/coach in the fashion of Imlach and Sinden. When Patrick was named general manager and coach of the St. Louis Blues expansion team, he selected Scotty Bowman as his assistant. Bowman had a good record in junior hockey, and had coached Patrick's son Craig. Bowman went on to a fabulous coaching career with St. Louis, when he succeeded Lynn in 1967; and later with Montreal, Pittsburgh, and Detroit. He became one of the most successful coaches in all sports. So Patrick can take credit for the careers of Imlach, Sinden, and Bowman.

Lynn Patrick kept a sharp eye on the Bruins budget. When I joined them in 1952, the team paid my expenses on the road. The train cost nothing because there was room for me on the Pullman car. On an early visit to Montreal, Patrick asked me if I really needed a hotel room. The club was staying at the Sheraton, and the players doubled up on each room rented for just a daytime stay. I said that I could get by without a room, and spent the day lounging in the lobby. Just before the players checked out to go to the game, I went to a room that Hal Laycoe and Jim Henry had occupied and had a shave and a shower. The arrangement made a very long day for me. Back in Boston, I protested to Walter Brown, the team president, and he told Lynn Patrick that henceforth I was to get a room. In all Patrick probably saved about 15 dollars on the Bruins budget by skimping on my accommodations.

Tom Johnson

Tom spent most of his playing career with the Montreal Canadiens in the late 1940s and 1950s. In his 15-year career, he was on a Stanley Cup-winning team six times. He was a Norris Trophy winner and member of the Hockey Hall of Fame. After playing two years with the Bruins, he moved into the front office, served a couple of years as coach (including a Stanley Cup win in 1972), and before retiring, served as vice president. For many years, he was a regular on road trips, and with his vast background in hockey, had many a story to tell as a dinner companion. After dinner, it was our usual pattern to return to the hotel lobby before heading back to our rooms. Hotel lobbies were a varied lot, and none were more elegant, nor had more old-world charm, than the lobby of the Chateau Frontenac in Quebec. Its steeply arching ceiling must have extended three floors high; richly woven Orientals graced the floor. At one end, a circular bar provided a sweeping view of the St. Lawrence River, and another smaller bar was located halfway down the lobby, almost discreetly hidden away. In the front of that bar was a Steinway, elegantly tuned, unlocked; and on weekends a professional played quietly for the entertainment of guests.

We were there one Thursday night, relaxing with a couple of good cigars when Tom Johnson asked me to play a tune or two. Now my piano playing is not something to brag about. My mother insisted that I take it up when I was about nine or ten, and I labored through it for several years with a variety of teachers who lamented my lack of practice and general indifference. But I did master some show tunes, which with some consistent practice, I could perform. "As Time Goes By," "Stardust," and "Begin the Beguine" were some of the standards.

Many of the tunes dated back to the '30s, and whenever I performed, no requests were honored. You heard my repertoire, and that was it. I moved the ashtray and the cigar over to the Steinway, and began my routine.

After about ten minutes, just as I was warming up, a tuxedoed gentleman who might have been an assistant manager came over and politely asked me to stop playing. I was running short of songs and the last thing I wanted to do was create a stir in the elegant hotel lobby. So I returned to where Tom Johnson was sitting. He beckoned the man who had told me to stop playing. He came over and Johnson introduced himself as a Bruins official in charge of the team's residence in the hotel. He further said that he wanted me to continue playing, and there was a subtle threat that the Bruins would be staying elsewhere if I didn't. The tuxedo didn't apologize (and didn't have to), but he waved me back to the piano and the concert continued.

Public Relations

The first full-time public relations director of the Boston Bruins was Nate Greenberg, who took over the job in 1974. Nate still handles the assignment, plus many more, as assistant to the president. In 1973 he handled PR for the Boston Braves of the American Hockey League. He succeeded Herb Ralby who was a sportswriter for *The Boston Globe* with a regular assignment covering the Boston Bruins in season. In order to handle the two jobs, Herb arranged for another sportswriter, Roger Barry, a hockey writer with *The Patriot Ledger*, to assist him. Basically, the two of them put out a daily news release. Surprisingly, I never heard a complaint from the other newspapers about the arrangement. Neither Herb nor Roger came up with any scoops to ruffle feathers in the media. It was standard procedure accepted by all the papers to allow moonlighting by their sportswriters and others.

Perhaps Frank Ryan, the first Bruins public relations director, had inured the hockey media to the practice. He might have been the premier moonlighter of all time, with five jobs on the side: a nightly sport program on WAAB, Bruins broadcasts on WNAC, city assessor in Boston, Suffolk Downs PR, and Harvard University sports PR. He ingratiated himself with the hockey media by initiating free Thursday night dinners before the game. They were held at the convenient Hotel Manger (later named the Madison) and were full-scale, sit-down meals. It established a practice adopted in varying degrees by all sports teams. For most, it is the largest item on their PR budget. Around the National Hockey League, the New York Rangers turned out an excellent spread. When Sonny Werblin took over as CEO of Madison Square Garden, he saw to it that the Rangers meal would be the best. Toronto used to have a decent collection of fancy sandwiches served in a not-too-spacious press room on the first floor; but when Harold Ballard took over ownership and quarreled with the Fourth Estate, he moved the free meal to the third floor, which meant a walk-up for the poorly conditioned media, and a collection of sandwiches that was anything but fancy. The Bruins' spread is a more-than-satisfactory buffet. Montreal moved into the Molson Centre and charged five dollars for their meal. This price would hardly break any of the media, but it was a slight shock to the writers, who had enjoyed freebies for decades.

Playoff time was a period when public relations men could really shine. The rubber band came off the team's bankroll, and food and drink were generously in evidence in the press suite of the hotel where the team was staying. The media for Boston was expanded to include representatives from radio, TV, and the press from all over New England. The press suite was open around the clock, except when the game was being played. The television sets might be on after the game, but usually it was conversation that dominated, including versions of controversial plays in the game, stories of past triumphs, and general hockey talk. The hometown press was also welcome, and the word hospitality was well defined every year in the playoffs.

For over 30 years, Nate Greenberg has proved to be one of the most popular and talented public relations men in the League. He arranged a picture and recognition of my 40 years broadcasting the Bruins by placing my photo on the cover of the press guide. At age 74, it was an honor.

CHAPTER NINE

The Big Bad Bruins and Others

Hockey is a great game to play—constant movement—everyone involved. Hockey requires agility, strength, stamina, and mental focus. So many New Englanders played the game on local ponds in the '20s, '30s, and '40s just as I had growing up, that there was a strong base of very knowledgeable fans—equal to Canada's. So, it was no surprise that with a catalyst like Orr, teamed with the likes of the Chief, Espo, Cheevers, and Derek Sanderson, that the teams of the early '70s ignited an even larger fan base.

The Chief

"Durability" is the word that comes to mind when writing about John Bucyk's hockey record. In 1958 the Bruins' Terry Sawchuck—one of hockey's great goaltenders—was traded back to Detroit for Bucyk. Ever since, "the Chief," as he was known, has been connected to the Bruins on and off the ice. He remained generally injury-free, playing a solid left wing for 21 years. In addition to his talent for scoring, his forechecking featured a skillful hip check that proved disconcerting to many a rival defenseman. First he joined Bronco Horvath and Vic Stasiak to form the UTE line. He scored 556 goals in his brilliant career. In 1970—a Stanley Cup year—he had 14 playoff goals. In 1972—another Stanley Cup year—he had 15 playoff goals. After his retirement in 1978, Bucyk became an analyst on Bruins radio broadcasts with Bob Wilson, and he was instrumental in the formation of the Boston Bruins Alumni Association.

Esposito

Phil Esposito was an awesome player for Boston. He was acquired (with Stanfield and Hodge) in a trade arranged by general manager Milt Schmidt. I believe it was one of the best trades the Bruins ever made. The trio formed a nucleus that joined Bobby Orr in producing the Stanley Cup victories in 1970 and 1972. They should have had one in 1971 after a season in which they stomped through the National Hockey League. That year, Esposito scored 76 goals and had 76 assists to lead the League. Up to that time, Bobby Hull held the record for goals scored in one season at 58. He was one shy going into a game in Los Angeles in March 1971. I knew Phil would break Hull's record that night. I was broadcasting the game alone on WBZ, and arranged for Ed Fitkin, a Los Angeles Kings PR man, to join me. Phil broke the record scoring two goals—59 and 60. I had brought along a tape recorder, and turning the play by play over to Fitkin, I hustled down 25 rows to the Bruins bench and startled Esposito by interviewing him while he was on the bench and the game was on. After a couple of minutes, I returned to the broadcast area and played the tape later. Esposito was happy with the result, and I was pleased with my ingenuity. It had to be an NHL first.

The Goaltenders

How important is the goaltender to a team? Some say as much as 70 percent, so a general manager better get a good one who can play consistently if his team is to have any success. In clutch situations, in "big money" games, Gerry Cheevers was the goaltender you wanted, and the Bruins had him for their Stanley Cup wins in 1970 and 1972. He had great mobility and he skated and moved the puck in his area like a third defenseman. He had been drafted by Toronto and the general manager/coach Punch Imlach tried to protect him on his roster by listing him as a forward. The Bruins were able to get him though, and it proved fortuitous. With the intrusion of the World Hockey Association, Cheevers was offered good money to play with Cleveland. The Bruins legal counsel, Charles Mulcahy, had tried negotiating a new contract with Cheevers in the midst of the important 1972 playoffs. Cheevers was annoyed, and that fact, as much as the money, led to his departure. He returned later not only to finish out his playing career, but also to coach the team.

When Cheevers left, the Bruins acquired Gilles Gilbert from Minnesota. Tall and agile, I thought he had the best skills to be a top-notch goaltender. He played well for Boston, but wasn't mentally prepared at all times, and it occasionally affected his play. Later, the Bruins secured Andy Moog from the Edmonton Oilers, where he was languishing behind Grant Fuhr. Andy was a first-string backstop who would challenge shooters and had good reflexes. When I first joined the Bruins in 1952, the goaltender was Jim Henry. He did not have much style, but somehow could stop the puck. Sometimes on long shots he would kneel down and place his stick across the ice in front of him and block the shot. It was effective, but not stylish. The players loved him, and that was the key. If the players have confidence in the goaltender, regardless of his mannerisms, the team is well on the road to success.

During his years with Boston, the team had great confidence in Reggie Lemelin. He was signed as a free agent in 1987 and won 24 games as he shared the backstop duties with Andy Moog. The combination combined to defeat Montreal enroute to the Stanley Cup finals. Two years later Reggie and Andy won the Jennings Trophy as the Bruins reached the finals for the second time in three years. Reggie is a regular at Bruins alumni games where he plays as a forward—the ambition of all goaltenders.

Unbelievably, the Bruins had Terry Sawchuck as their goaltender in the seasons 1955–56 and 1956–57 (he played in only 38 games the second year). He is arguably the greatest goaltender of the 20th century. He had all sorts of records with a powerhouse Detroit team, and until his collapse from stress and erratic behavior, had elevated the fortunes of the Bruins. After his early retirement, Detroit brought him back, and he wound up in Toronto, where in 1967, in combination with Johnny Bower, he backstopped the Maple Leafs to a Stanley Cup win.

The two great 20th-century goaltender stories involved Johnny Bower and Lorne "Gump" Worsley. Bower was born in 1924 and began his professional career with Cleveland of the American Hockey League in 1945. Ten years later, he was still in the League with Providence, and the coach was Jack Crawford. I recall Jack telling me about his goaltender, Bower, how talented he was, and how content he was in being a top-notch AHL net minder. That ended in 1958 when Punch Imlach took over as general manager of the Toronto Maple Leafs. He drafted Bower in what seemed like a ridiculous move, since the goaltender was 34 years old. Imlach knew what he was doing. In 11 seasons with the Maple Leafs, Bower did a superb job. The veteran team won the Stanley Cup four times in 1962, '63, '64, and '67.

Gump Worsley was a similar story. He was a rookie goaltender with the New York Rangers in the 1952–53 season. They were a poor team, and his record was 13 wins, 29 losses, and eight ties. Incredibly, he was named Rookie of the Year, winning the Calder Trophy. His career with the lowly Rangers in the 1950s was a difficult one. The team gave Worsley plenty of practice, giving up 40 or more shots in many games. Phil Watson was the coach during one stretch, and he forbade Worsley from leaving the net and wandering behind the cage to handle the puck. To restrain him during practice sessions, he actually tied a rope around Worsley. But the team's misfortunes were not the goaltender's fault—the talent in front of him was just not there. That was proven in 1963 when Worsley was traded to the Montreal Canadiens. Talk about going from the outhouse to the penthouse. Two years later, Montreal won the Stanley Cup. Overall, in seven seasons with the team, the Canadiens won four Stanley Cups with Worsley. The Gumper wound up his 25-year professional career with Minnesota, retiring in 1974.

Speaking of Phil Watson, after failing as the Rangers coach, he was hired by Lynn Patrick to coach the Bruins. Phil thought he had solved a big problem at the start of the 1962 season. The Bruins were in the doldrums, going through a stretch where they would not make the playoffs for eight consecutive years. They opened their season at home against the Montreal Canadiens, and Watson decided that a rolypoly goaltender name Bob Perrault would start in the nets. He didn't look like a goaltender, and as a matter of fact, did not look like an athlete. He had spent several years in the Montreal organization, but being a backup for Jacques Plante did not provide much work. The Bruins hopped to a 2–0 lead against the powerful Canadiens, and Perrault came through with sensational stops on Belliveau and the Pocket Rocket Richard. Boston added to its lead, and Perrault and his teammates wound up with a 5–0 victory. It looked as though Boston was on its way to the playoffs; but in subsequent appearances, Perrault reverted to his minor-league form, and won only three games in 20 appearances. Eddie Johnston took over the first string role.

There are those who would argue that Jacques Plante of the Montreal Canadiens was just as good as Sawchuck. He won six Stanley Cups with Montreal. He, of course, was the first to wear a mask, despite the strong objection of his coach Toe Blake. Plante insisted, and soon every goaltender in the NHL was masked. It seemed odd that Plante, so much a nemesis of the Bruins, would wind up with the team at the end of his career. He is best remembered for how, when Boston won, he would skate off at the end of the game, pause as he was about to leave the ice, and make a graceful pirouette as he waved to the fans. It was unique and memorable.

The Substitute

His name is not listed in the Boston Bruins all-time roster, but for 13 years, John Aiken was an integral part of the organization. The Arlington, Massachusetts, native practiced regularly with the team and attended every home game as the spare net minder.

In the National Hockey League's six-team era, there were only six goaltenders. Each team was required to have a standby at home games should an emergency occur. He would sit in the stands and was on call if something happened to either the visitor's or the home team's goaltender.

Inevitably, it happened, and John Aiken was part of a memorable night on March 13, 1958. Jacques Plante, like the other five goaltenders, played without a mask. (A year later he was to don one permanently, and the other goaltenders soon followed). Early in the second period of the Bruins-Montreal game, Plante sustained a concussion in a three-way collision with Doug Harvey, and Bruin forward Vic Stasiuk. The call went out to Aiken. Within minutes, he was putting on the historic colors of the rouge, blanc et bleu. A warm-up was allowed, and soon he was handling shots from Rocket Richard, Jean Beliveau, Tom Johnson, and others. Despite the reassurances of these famous colleagues, he was a very nervous goaltender.

Aiken had been All-Scholastic at Arlington High School, a standout at West Point, and after transferring to Boston University, had turned in a solid season with the Terriers. His résumé included six years of practice work with the Bruins, but this was the real thing. The Canadiens were a powerhouse, and in the middle of a five-year run of Stanley Cup titles. As Aiken entered the game, the Bruins led 1–0.

Boston erupted for five goals in the second period, as sharpshooters like Peirson, Horvath, and Bucyk were able to capitalize on their knowledge of the new Canadien goaltender. They had practiced with him so many times they knew his every move. The final score was 7–3 for the Bruins. John Aiken was understandably upset at the outcome. A letter from Frank Selke, the managing director of the Canadiens, brought some consolation and a check for $100. Mr. Selke said: "No matter what the results were we admired your courage and keen desire to help us win."

Selke, of course, was the shrewd manipulator of the Montreal franchise who made sure that his team led the League in all departments. The Canadiens fostered a draft rule that allowed them territorial rights to French players in the Province of Quebec. The Bruins had a superb prospect in goaltender Phil Myre. They were set to draft him out of junior hockey when the Canadiens stepped in, and said that since he was of French descent, they would take him. The French connection was quite a reach, but they made it stand up. Myre was to turn in 14 very good years in the National Hockey League.

The Bruins were part of another "backup goaltender" affair with Montreal. On January 14, 1956, they had called up John Henderson from Hershey to play a game in Montreal. Henderson arrived, but his equipment did not—particularly his size-14 skates. The Bruins had to ask the Canadiens for a substitute. There were plenty of replacements in the Montreal area, and Selke went deep into his system and came up with junior goaltender Claude Pronovost. In a stunning turn of events, the young goaltender backstopped the Bruins to a 2–0 win. He played a couple of years in the Montreal organization, but had little chance for regular work with the indomitable Jacques Plante well underway toward a Hall of Fame career.

John Aiken did not duplicate the Pronovost performance, but he stayed with the Bruins for seven more years. Off the ice, he pursued a career as a mathematician and engineer at Hanscom Air Force Base. At Electronic Systems Division he supervised computer operations at "Space Track," a high-priority project for keeping a defensive eye on every manmade object orbiting Earth. During the Cold War, it was an integral part of our defense. Now retired and living in Billerica, Massachusetts, Aiken can tell Cold War stories to his grandchildren about tracking satellites or begin one with the phrase, "And then there was the night I played goal for the Montreal Canadiens…"

The Fighters

Boston Garden was built for boxing and hockey. Pro basketball as we know it today did not exist. So perhaps it is natural that through their history, the Bruins were known as a tough, combative team just as willing to drop their gloves as they were ready to score goals. Fighting has been a part of the game since it began, and for the most part, fights are among players who have earned "tough-guy" reputations. Paul Pender, a boxing champion, enjoyed watching hockey and he commented to me, "I don't know how they do it. Hockey players are on skates, they're wearing shoulder pads, yet the good ones can throw punches with abandon."

Pender's particular favorite was Terry O'Reilly, but then, O'Reilly was everybody's favorite. After 13 hardscrabble years with the team, and three more as the coach, he fittingly had his number 24 retired. At 6-foot-1 and 200 pounds, he was a second choice and 14th overall, for the Bruins after steadily improving during his three-year stint with the Oshawa Generals. Oshawa had been the proving ground of Bobby Orr and Wayne Cashman, so Bruins fans were encouraged by the pick. Cashman was a player who you wanted on the ice when things became rough and tumble, and he played on the first line, so he created a lot of ice room for partners Esposito and Hodge. But O'Reilly had another dimension. When he came up, he was a poor skater, so he constantly worked on improving that skill. He seemed to have endless endurance, acquired by punishing practice sessions that went well beyond whatever the coach required. In the 1977–78 season it paid off, as O'Reilly had 29 goals and 61 assists—a fabulous season for a player who was also compiling over 200 minutes in penalties. In fact, he had over 200 minutes in penalties for five consecutive years. Another player in the O'Reilly mold was John Wensink. He was the same size, and play-making and scoring were not high on his list of talents. He had some memorable fights, but his role in a game was not as active as O'Reilly's, so his penalty minutes never reached 200—his highest was 181. He had one good scoring year, though, when he posted 28 goals in 1977–78.

In 1975, the Bruins drafted a player who might rank as the National Hockey League's all-time best puncher. Stan Jonathan, at 5-foot-8 and 180 pounds could punch like Rocky Marciano. He played for five years, and his best one was 1977–78. He scored 27 goals and had 25 assists, playing on a line with Greg Sheppard at center and Don Marcotte on the other wing. Sheppard was a good playmaker, and Marcotte was a splendid two-way wing who would always take care of the back checking. Obviously, as his fighting reputation spread, Jonathan created a lot of room on left wing and in front of the net. In a 1980 game with the Canadiens, Jonathan became entangled with defenseman Pierre Bouchard, the son of legendary Montreal defenseman Butch Bouchard. At 6-foot-2 and 195 pounds, Pierre had been a stalwart on the Canadiens blue line. As the two fought, they became separated from the brawling teams, and were on open ice, toe to toe. The smaller Jonathan uncorked a haymaker that landed squarely on Bouchard's jaw and sent him crumbling to the ice. In all the years of all the fights that hockey fans had seen, there was never anything quite like this one. Jonathan's reputation as a phenomenal puncher was made.

Decades later, the interest in this episode, and other famous hockey fights continues. YouTube—the popular video web portal—features many hockey fights. The Jonathan/Bouchard confrontation, featuring my commentary, has been viewed thousands of times by hockey fans around the world.

Another fighter during the days of the Big Bad Bruins, was my future broadcasting partner, Derek Sanderson. In the 1972 series, he was instrumental in stirring up animosity from the New York Rangers. It paid off in a Bruins Stanley Cup victory. Eventually, the game took a toll on Derek. When he worked with me in 1990s, the long walk up to the broadcast booth was difficult due to his two artificial hips, but he never gave up sports. Years later, Derek proved a valuable partner in lining up golf play in some of the best courses in North America. He still played the game with a low handicap, and was able to hit the ball a long way, despite the hips.

Nifty—Rick Middleton

Hockey players are big on nicknames. Most of them developed from a modification of the last name—Esposito became "Espo," and Cashman became "Cash." Others have unknown origins. In their early years, one of the most talented and popular players for over 20 years was Aubrey "Dit" Clapper. With a moniker like Aubrey, it was logical that someone would come up with a nickname. For some mysterious reason, a contemporary of Clapper's, Ralph Weiland, was always known as "Cooney." Some well-known players never had a nickname, Bobby Orr among them. Rounding out some spectacular scoring feat, I would say "Number four, Bobby Orr." One of the best nicknames was "Rocket" Richard. I always called him that, never Maurice.

One of the finest forwards in Bruins history came to the team in 1976 in a trade with the New York Rangers. Rick Middleton was traded for Ken Hodge. Rick had some indifferent seasons with the Rangers, but completing his career with the Bruins in 1988, he hung up some impressive numbers. But it wasn't the numbers so much as the way he did it. Fans had filled the old Garden watching the spectacular play of Bobby Orr. Later, when Middleton arrived on the scene, he became known as a player to watch. Game after game, he demonstrated stick handling and skating talent that brought fans out of their seats. He often climaxed his maneuvers with a head-to-head meeting with the rival goaltender. Many times, Middleton would win the matchup by either drawing the goaltender out of position or, if he held the fort, picking a spot and firing it into the net. Someone called him "Nifty," and the nickname stuck. The dictionary says that nifty means one who is smart, stylish, and clever. Rick Middleton was all of those.

The Bruins held to the Canadien practice of picking three stars for each game played. At the end of the season a prize went to the player who was selected the No. 1 star the most times. For six years in a row, Rick Middleton was named THE No. 1 star for the season. He was generally regarded as the best one-on-one player in the League. This unique talent led him to rank fourth in the all-time Bruins scoring totals behind Bourque, Bucyk, and Esposito. In 881 games, he had 402 goals and 496 assists. Because of his talent, he would draw tight coverage by the opposition, and this was accented in the playoffs. His playoff record is just as good as his regular season. He had 45 goals and 55 assists for a total of 100 points in 111 games. He ranks fourth on the Bruins' all-time list of scorers in playoffs.

He became a commentator on Bruins games in pre- and postgame shows, and plays for the Bruins Alumni as they make charitable appearances around New England. He is still a top attraction, handling the puck and making moves—and non-moves—that were an integral part of his play in his active days. Players of far lesser talent have been named to the Hall of Fame. At the least, Rick Middleton deserves a Bruins honor—retiring his number 16.

The Great One

Ninety-two goals in a season is hard to ignore—but in the controversy over whom would you pick—I would take Orr over "the Great One."

Wayne Gretzky was a finesse player with incredible peripheral vision. He could see the game as no one else could—except Bobby Orr. He was tall and slender, weighing around 175 pounds and never had to use a physical style past his preteen days. Like Orr, he exhibited a ton of class both on and off the ice.

Teammates gladly took up the burden of back-checking and taking care of the contact side of the game for Wayne. There was an unwritten law in the National Hockey League during Gretzky's tenure: If you hit Wayne—even legally—you do so at your own peril.

Glen Sather, the wily general manager of the Edmonton Oilers, hired Dave Semenko, at 6-foot-2, 220 pounds, to take care of all the protection that Gretzky would need. Wayne got his share of points and goals at Boston Garden, but it was not one of his favorite arenas.

It was a shorter rink than others, and with an intimidating crowd intimately positioned to be a vocal factor in the game.

In an Oiler-Bruins regular-season game, John Blum (a brother-in-law to Mark Messier, a brilliant Edmonton forward) inadvertently caught Gretzky in a solid body check at center ice. It was perfectly legal, but a violation of the code: "Don't touch Wayne." For the rest of the game, Semenko and company (including Messier) never let Blum forget it. They were all over him in retaliation for hitting their prized possession. Blum, who was 6-foot-2, 210 pounds, could take care of himself, and he handled it well. No riot ensued, and Gretzky went on to play his usual slick game.

Gretzky might well be called a "floater." Many a time at the Boston Garden, he lurked out at the red line, while his teammates and the Bruins battled desperately in the Edmonton zone. Suddenly, an Oiler would get possession, pass it up to Gretzky at the red line, and a devastating offense would be underway. He would make those flawless lead passes to where a teammate was going to be, or, operating from behind the net as though he owned the territory, he would set up teammates for sure-fire scoring chances.

For those who saw hockey in the original six-team league, there remains the question of how Gretzky would do in that venue. How would Hall of Famer, Milt Schmidt of the Boston Bruins have handled him head-to-head? Milt played a physical game, and his defensive talent matched his scoring ability. Gretzky might well have been a top scorer and point-getter, as Rocket Richard was at the time, but he would have had to pay a physical price. The Schmidts and Howes of that era were not intimidated by the threat of a Dave Semenko-type of player. There were players of that time who relished the body-contact phase of the game.

Gretzky the Greatest? I will enter a demure. Bobby Orr could control the game more from his defense position—and do so at any speed. He set the tempo. Gordie Howe, with his physical presence, simply dominated his lane and cleared a path for himself and his teammates. Bobby Hull could shake off the close and at times illegal checking of a Provost (Canadiens), Westfall (Bruins), and score a flock of goals. Milt Schmidt would welcome the challenge; and Mario Lemieux, who as a big man had to endure the physical intimidation that Gretzky never received, was more involved in the game. They were players who contributed as much to the game as Gretzky. I'd pick all five ahead of him, but it's very hard to pass up that 92-goal season. Now Gretzky is a coach, and he must wonder at times what he could do under today's rules. He would be "floating" up at the blue line instead of center ice, and he would have scoring opportunities galore.

CHAPTER TEN

More Bruins Musings and Retirement

Normand Leveille

One of the great skills in hockey—for which no statistics are kept—is body checking. Some coaches like to keep track of the number of hits their team makes in a game, but that includes just about any contact that a player makes against his opponent.

In their early years, the Bruins had a solidly built defenseman, Jack Crawford, who dealt devastating checks that slowed down many a forward. When he retired, he joined me in the broadcast booth for a couple of years and kept an eye on hard-hitting players who could throw their weight around. Jack said that it was just a knack that some players had. It took perfect timing and was most effective when an opponent had his head down. Later the Bruins had a stocky defenseman, Leo Boivin. He was only about 5-foot-8 and 200 pounds, but he could deal terrific body checks. He was generally recognized as about the best of all time, and the fans at Boston

Garden loved him. Until Leveille came, Milt Schmidt and John Bucyk had been the best Bruins body-checking forwards.

In 1981, the Bruins had a first-round draft choice, but they were number 14 on the list. They selected a slightly built forward, Normand Leveille, who was 5-foot-10 and weighed 175 pounds. At 18 years and five months of age, he was the youngest player ever drafted by the Bruins, but he had hung up impressive scoring credentials at Chicoutimi in the Quebec Junior League—he had 55 goals and 46 assists. There was no advance notice that he had other skills, but it was soon discovered at training camp that he had a talent for body checking.

Most forwards don't spend much effort on body checking; they know that the big money is in scoring. Players agree that body checking is a unique skill that is nearly impossible to learn—a player either has it or he doesn't. Leveille was a natural body checker. He knew how to do it and when to do it. He was able to deliver what one Bruins coach, Don Cherry, would call a "knock them on their ass" body check. As a forechecker, Leveille took on any-sized defenseman he could. The fans in Boston were thrilled. Their cheers would explode in the intimate Boston Garden setting.

Leveille was equally effective on the road. I have a vivid memory of broadcasting a game at Chicago Stadium. Bob Murray was a highly talented Blackhawk defenseman who had a 15-year career with the team. On one shift, Leveille forechecked Murray in the Blackhawk end of the ice and flattened him with a solid hit. Play resumed, and within a minute Murray had the puck in the Chicago corner again. Leveille moved in on him and knocked him down with a clean, hard body check. In all my years covering professional hockey, I never saw that duplicated—two "knock him down" hits in about a minute.

Game in, game out, Leveille continued his body checking. He did it so efficiently that it never caused fights, nor did it cause any injury to Leveille. As a rookie in 75 games, Leveille scored 17 goals, but everybody was talking about his body checking.

The fans could hardly wait for another season to begin; however, they wouldn't be getting what they expected. On October 23, 1982, the Bruins were playing in Vancouver. Leveille had complained of severe headaches before the game, but he played anyway. He had to leave the game. The cause was a brain aneurysm. It was not the result of any game injury, rather a defective blood vessel in his brain. It took a seven-hour operation to save his life, and his hockey career was finished. The fact that he was in superb condition when the tragedy struck is probably the only reason that he survived.

At the closing ceremonies at the Boston Garden on September 28, 1995, Leveille skated with Raymond Bourque in one of the most memorable scenes in the old rink's history. Fans remembered the tremendous talent and unique skill that an unkind fate had ended. They cheered for his great resolve to make something of his life. Leveille is an advocate and fundraiser for the disabled. He focuses his efforts on a 200-acre recreational area for people with disabilities in Quebec that is named after him. He has learned to drive a car, and hit golf balls. There's only one year of major league play in his résumé, but it is one that Bruins fans will never forget.

Bruins Alumni

In 1968, the Bruins started an alumni association when they realized that New England was solid hockey country and many of their retired players continued to live in the area. Since its founding, the association has raised more than $5 million for charities and youth hockey programs. Fundraisers are mainly during the winter months, when a team of alumni, dressed in Bruins uniforms, takes on a local team made up of firemen or policemen, for example. It is a non-body-checking affair. While the pace is not fast, the alumni still demonstrate their individual skills. It is difficult, though, for a Terry O'Reilly to show off his body-checking talent.

In the summer, at a well-organized golf tournament, loyal Bruins fans complete foursomes with a Bruins alumnus. Thousands of dollars are raised for charity, and there is great camaraderie and enjoyment for the participants. Individually, Alumni members play in hundreds of local charity events as celebrity invitees. Led by Bobby Orr, a long roster of former players has found that living in New England provides them with the comforting warmth of remembrance and recognition. When Orr appears with the alumni at charity events, he is restricted to coaching and not playing; his knees continue to be a problem. There are many Bruins alumni who live in the Greater Boston area year round.

Neely and Bourque

I had the pleasure of calling all the games played by Neely and Bourque. Imagine what it was like for opposing teams to see those two players line up on the right side of the ice. Bourque generally played right defense, but one of his greatest assets was that he could also play left defense with equal skill. With Cam and Ray on the right side, you could envision a clear track to the opponent's goal—Neely leading the way with his physical presence. Body checking was a big part of his game, though when needed, he could stick handle like teammate Rick Middleton. The climax? A thunderous shot that went directly into the back of the net.

Playoff action was close checking and hard hitting. Neely thrived on it. No Bruin has scored more goals in playoff action than Neely. Ray Bourque, a Hall of Famer like Neely, was one of the most durable players in National Hockey League history. As team captain, he led by example. He was on hand after every game to give the media his analysis of what happened and was available even if the Bruins had lost the game.

In my last year of broadcasting, after having played a game in Quebec, we went to board the charter jet that awaited us at the airport. Unfortunately, it was parked way out, and it meant at least a quarter-mile walk from the gate. I was carrying my luggage plus a heavy bag loaded with books that belonged to Derek Sanderson, the TV analyst, who was studying for a broker's license. He couldn't carry it because of his two artificial hips. At age 77, I had volunteered to carry them.

The media preceded the players on the long walk to the flight, and as I walked ahead, I started to slow down with the twin burdens. I finally had to stop for a rest. Walking behind, Bourque noticed my plight. He quietly came up and picked up the bag of books and then carried them the rest of the way to the plane. A small gesture, to be sure, but a big relief for an aging sportscaster. Bourque had two outstanding qualities on the ice: his durability and his consistently high level of play. He could carry the puck or set up a scoring play with a deft pass to a teammate. He was the man you wanted on the ice in the closing minutes of a game when the Bruins were protecting a one-goal lead.

Helping other people was a way of living that Ray Bourque embraced. He partnered with a variety of defensemen in his long career, and his talented play made them better players. Bourque is a class act.

Fittingly, Neely was inducted into the Hockey Hall of Fame on November 7, 2005. He had compiled an enviable record over a 10-year career with the Bruins. Like Orr, injuries cropped up that had him spending as much time in the trainer's room as he did on the ice. Despite a thigh injury, and later a knee injury, he turned in a superb season in 1993–94. In just 44 games, he scored 50 goals. It is one of the greatest goal-scoring feats in the history of the NHL. Game in and game out, he continued his hard-hitting, aggressive play that created so many scoring opportunities. Neely's play was limited the following season, and he missed 32 of the final 35 games. In 1995–96, he retired. Living in the Boston area, he turned his attention to the formation of the Neely Foundation. In 1995, in association with Tufts New England Medical Center, the foundation set up facilities to accommodate the overwhelming needs of cancer patients' families. Since its start, the Neely Foundation has raised over $15 million and helped many families.

I often wondered what opponents must have thought as they watched Neely and Bourque line up on the right side to start a game—Neely at right wing and Bourque at right defense. They owned that area of the rink.

Blockbuster

The definition of blockbuster is "overwhelmingly impressive, effective or influential"; and this trade filled those three requirements.

The Bruins traded Phil Esposito and Carol Vadnais to the New York Rangers for Brad Park, Jean Ratelle, and Joe Zanussi. It shook up the hockey world, and particularly the fans in Boston and New York. Esposito thought he would never be traded, and Park and Ratelle figured they were lifetime players for the Rangers. It happened on November 7, 1975, and the experts were quick to offer their analyses. Most thought that the Rangers got the better of the deal, but in the end, the Bruins fared better.

Brad Park was a known threat because he was ranked right behind Orr in all-around talent. Ratelle was rated a good player, but he turned out to be an excellent one. In a head-to-head matchup with Esposito, he scored more points with the Bruins than Esposito did with the Rangers. His greatest asset was consistency—he always played with a high level of talent. Looking back at Ratelle's Ranger record, Bruins fans discovered that in the 1971–72 season he compiled 109 points playing between two top scorers in Vic Hatfield and Rod Gilbert. His +/- rating was plus 61. Sadly, Park only played 10 games with Bobby Orr because the latter's injuries caught up with him. With Park and Ratelle making large contributions to the cause, the Bruins went to the Stanley Cup finals in 1977 and 1978. Park signed with the Detroit Red Wings in 1983 and finished his career with them.

Away from the game, both Park and Ratelle found Boston an excellent hockey city. They established homes in the area and raised their children there. Well into retirement, they still live there. Ratelle is one of the finest golfers among a coterie of ex-players who have taken up the game. Park plays well. Both participate in charity events, many of them sponsored by the Boston Bruins Alumni Association.

The Lowell Lock Monsters

I retired from the Bruins broadcasts in 1997. I was contacted by Chris Miller, a television producer for MediaOne, a cable network. We had tried to produce programs for cable that would be commercially successful, among them, *New England Sports Legends.* We even made a TV pilot with Jim Craig who was the goaltender of the "Miracle on Ice" Olympic team of 1980, but we were unable to get it on the air. Chris wondered if I would be interested in doing the play-by- play of American Hockey League games in Lowell, Massachusetts. A new team was being formed and they would play in the new state-of-the-art Tsongas Arena. The network planned to cover 12 games, and Miller, very talented in all phases of television, would be the producer. I told him I would do it, and he asked who should be the analyst. Without hesitation, I said Brad Park, who was delighted with the opportunity.

The Lowell Lock Monsters, as they were known, held a press conference with Brad and me in attendance. I told the Lowell press that this would not be my first broadcast event in the city. In 1962, I had called a Boston Patriots and New York Titans (now Jets) football game from the Lowell High School stadium on WEEI. There were 11,000 fans on hand, and Howard Cosell provided the New York radio coverage. Because of a crowded press box, he had to sit outside the booth and just in front of our WEEI setup. From time to time, I could hear him as he interviewed Sonny Werblin, who was about to take over the team from the financially strapped Harry Wismer and rename them the Jets. Howard was very much a homer, and in no way offered the controversial comments that were often a highlight of

Monday Night Football. The fans paid no attention to him because he was not an ABC television personality yet.

The Lowell hockey broadcast area was ideal. A center ice seat about 20 rows high in the press box was just about perfect. Brad Park added to the broadcast with his keen analysis. He prepared diligently. For the last couple of years in our partnership, he had a laptop computer with complete information on every player in professional hockey. Listening to him, I could not understand why he was not a coach in the National Hockey League. He had spent some time as a scout for the New York Rangers, a team that was floundering under the direction of Glen Sather.

In all, I was with Park for five years. We covered the Lowell team in addition to a new one in Manchester, New Hampshire. Park prepared for the games by interviewing the coaches and drawing charts that contained information on the players performing that night. Broadcasting the games was exciting—the energy and enthusiasm of the crowd were contagious.

MediaOne sold out to AT&T, which was later bought out by Comcast. I ended my hockey play-by-play career in 2002 at age 83—not a bad run for a sportscaster.

CHAPTER ELEVEN

Scooooore!

The dean of hockey broadcasters, Foster Hewitt, used the phrase "he shoots, he scores" as his trademark description of a goal. His son, Bill, who succeeded him on TV, used the same four words. I was never really aware of what I used, but more often than not, I would just use the one word: "Score!" or "He scores!" Sometimes, if it were a spectacular goal made by an Orr or Neely, I would drag out the word for four or five seconds. That was the signal that it was special. I never did that consciously—it was just something that developed.

That one word—"score"—paid off for me handsomely when Bobby Orr made a 30-second commercial for Mastercard that was only televised in Canada. The beginning of the commercial showed Bobby scoring a goal, and had me announcing "Score!" The second part had Orr sinking a putt. McCann-Erickson, Mastercard's advertising agency, sent me a sample of the commercial, and asked if it was my voice on the tape. When I assured them that it was my voice, I started to receive $158 checks in regular cycles. Not bad for one word.

If the game was on the road, there would not be much of a crowd reaction to a Boston goal, so I would try to fill the gap by pointing out who got the assists. John Peirson would come in immediately and describe the setup to the goal and tell the fans what to watch for. He was uncanny in his ability to describe what had happened to create the goal before he saw the replay.

Sometimes people listening to a game don't realize the difference between doing a home game and a road game. If the Bruins were winning on the road, the hometown fans could hardly be heard. My voice would be down a notch, and some people would think that I didn't show sufficient enthusiasm. Not so, there was just no point in yelling when there wasn't any background support from the crowd.

There is one game in particular where a Bruins executive's reaction to my play-by-play is particularly memorable. The Bruins were in front by three goals, but the Pittsburgh Penguins exploded, urged on by a packed house. Led by Lowell MacDonald, Syl Apps, and Jean Pronovost, they scored four times and won the game. The sellout crowd at the Igloo was ecstatic. In order to be heard over their thunderous cheers, I had to raise my voice to its peak. To the Bruins executive listening in Boston, it sounded like I was rooting for the Penguins. Nothing could be further from the truth. It was straightforward reporting.

Occasionally, when I'm out and about, a Bruins fan will talk with me. Invariably our talk will turn to Bobby Orr. Usually, their one request is asking me to re-create a Bobby Orr goal. "Come on, Fred…give us a SCOOORE!" I am always happy to oblige.

Game Day

In the 1970s, my family moved to Cape Cod. My two oldest had graduated from college—Martha from the University of Wisconsin and Ted from Bowdoin. Sarah matriculated to Princeton, and Mary was still in high school but on her way to Yale after graduation.

I had a regular routine for broadcasting home games. The commute from Cape Cod meant allowing for an hour-and-a-half drive to Boston. As I neared the city, most of the traffic was headed south, so I seldom experienced delays. I arrived at the parking lot opposite the Garden by about 5:30 p.m. for a 7:30 p.m. game. I would head for the press room and pick up the all-encompassing stat sheet, which would contain complete information on both teams involved in the game. A meal would be served, and while enjoying it I found that the best information on the visiting team could be obtained from that club's broadcasters. They'd tell you who was injured, who was playing well, and who was playing poorly. Many times the visiting coach would be in the press room. While most were amiable, they tended not to give out anything that could be classified as information about their team.

A half hour before the opening face-off, the teams would come out for a 15-minute warm-up. During that time I spent my most productive moments in the broadcast booth, insuring that I knew the name and numbers of every player on the visiting team, and making careful note of their line and defense combinations as they worked out. Occasionally, the director would want the opening recorded while the teams were working out; or perhaps would want to have a promotion piece taped, but I tried to discourage the practice.

Unlike other sports, a hockey game moves rapidly and there isn't time to present long-winded stories about the players or other team personnel. When the telecasts started in the early '50s in Canada, there was great concern about how commercials would be handled. At the start, three 20-second commercials were allowed in each period. A red light was installed next to the penalty box and when it was lit, it was a signal to the referee that it was commercial break time. The director in the truck called them. He would indicate it to me on the intercom by saying, "We'll take a time out on the next whistle." For games in Canada, the CBC controlled the telecast and called the breaks. For other U.S. cities, except New York, the home games were not televised locally.

After the game, I would go to the locker room and talk to the coach as well as available players. Sometimes there was a controversial play that a player wanted to clear up, and he wanted my opinion on what the television replay showed. I'd stay in the locker room until I was sure that the traffic had cleared up. I would listen to the car radio on my way home in order to find out about the results of other hockey games.

Road games provided the same opportunities, and the team's hotel was always the base of operations. The team bus left the hotel in time to give the players about two hours' arrival time before the game. I was on that bus every road game.

No "F" Word

I began my Bruins play-by-play career in 1952, and a couple of years later a new media area was created on the overhang of the first balcony. The print press was located on the north side, and the broadcasters on the south. Both areas provided the best seats in the house, and drew the plaudits of visitors from around the League. There was only one problem—the cleaning crews at the Garden would frequently leave the mess that would accumulate. At least that was the situation in the south side—I was never in the print-press area. If no cleaning had been done over a period of a week, there would be a fair accumulation of score sheets, gum wrappers, gum, box tops, and other debris scattered among permanent television cables.

In 1992, I had a new crown inserted to solve a dental problem. In the process, the dentist gave me a temporary crown. In no way did it affect my broadcasting. At a game against the Montreal Canadiens, I was preparing to pick up the play-by-play in the third period. Between periods, and all the time I was in my broadcast seat, I made it a rule not to eat or drink anything. Getting to the bathroom facilities at the Garden Club (using the public bathrooms was out of the question) at intermission—through the crowded aisles—was almost impossible. It was better to wait until after the game. On this particular night, our assistant director had brought some candy, and on an impulse I took a caramel that seemed particularly appealing. I was chewing on it when it stuck in my temporary crown. I panicked and hastily grabbed at the candy, pulled it out, and tossed it below the desk in what proved to be a pile of rubbish. I quickly realized, however, that I had pulled out the temporary crown with the candy.

There was a gap in my upper row of teeth! Could I talk intelligibly? I cupped my ears and tested. Yes the voice was OK, but there was a problem. If a word began with "f," I could not pronounce it. But the score was 4–2 for the Bruins—how could I give the regular cue for a commercial: "We're in the third period with the score Boston, 4, and Montreal, 2?" The "f" in four could not be heard. So

I changed it to: "We're in the third period, and Boston leads by 2." Until the end of the game I had to be conscious of not using any word with "f" in it. You can bet there were no face-offs. And I was delighted that Ferny Flaman had long been retired. I managed to get through the game and made a quick, non-smiling wrap up. To this day, no one but my family knows of the event, and yes, I was able to recover the temporary crown before the next game. The cleaners had not been around, and by going up to the broadcast area very early, and with the help of cameraman Joe Karras, who had a flashlight, I was able to spot the temporary crown.

The ADs

AD in television stands for the assistant director. He or she coordinates the flow of information between the announcer and the director in the truck. They are also to keep a record of goals and assists. When I first started broadcasting Bruins games, I quickly discovered that it would be beneficial to have an assistant who would keep track of the statistics. When a goal was scored, it was important to be able to recap the goal, who received the assists, and the time. I could not hear the official announcement because our location was virtually in the stands, and I was still doing play-by-play. On occasion it was important to get the exact cause of the penalty and the time. I hired my nephew, John Cusick, who was in high school; and later my brother-in-law, Dick Mullin, who was also a high school student, to keep track of the figures. On the road, the publicity man of the home team usually provided an assistant to help me out.

The best person at this assignment in my experience had been Joe Costanza, although he never worked Bruins games. When I was sports director of WVOM, broadcasting a whole range of sporting events, Joe would be alongside not only with up-to-the-second statistics, but with researched background information. When Curt Gowdy came to Boston to broadcast the Red Sox, Joe interviewed for the job as an assistant and was hired. He made a career out of it by joining Gowdy when he did football games, as well on NBC-TV. When Gowdy left football, Joe Costanza had compiled such a marvelous record that he stayed on as a major part of the network broadcast team. Accurate football statistics enhanced the broadcast, but they were more difficult to handle and come by than baseball. Figuring out the number of first downs was easy, but how about net yardage gained on the ground by one of the teams? I hired Costanza to help me when I was assigned by CBS radio to cover a Boston College-Boston University football game at Fenway Park. The network had Red Barber host a roundup of scores and highlights of games around the country. The following summer, Vin Scully joined Red Barber in the Dodgers' radio booth and went on to one of the most distinguished careers in broadcasting.

I made eight live reports from Boston with Joe Costanza providing me with vital information. They were about two minutes in length. At half time, the home team provided an array of statistics, but I needed up-to-date information during the game, because Barber could call on me at anytime. To say that Joe Costanza was invaluable is an understatement. Later, Joe revealed an on-air talent at WHDH, joining a panel of newspapermen for a round table half-hour discussion. Listeners were astounded at his vast knowledge of all sports.

That Saturday, I had taken the football assignment because I was sports director of WEEI, a CBS affiliate; but I had another job—

Bruins play-by-play broadcaster on WHDH. The Bruins were in Montreal that night. I figured that with the help of Northeast Airlines I could do both jobs. It was a gamble. I was able to leave the football game with about five minutes left to play, and that enabled me to beat the traffic out of Fenway and make the five o'clock flight to Montreal. It ran on schedule, and a cab from the Montreal Airport sped me to the Forum. Game traffic at the Forum proved to be an obstacle, but I got out of the cab and ran the last 200 yards, making it to my broadcast booth in the nick of time. Doing the game was easy—it was just getting there that proved to be the hurdle. In one day though, I had broadcast a college football game and a hockey game.

At TV38, a variety of people handled the job of assistant director. Their primary assignment was to coordinate the commercials from the studio and the commercial cues from the Garden. Their secondary duty was to record the statistics on goals, assists, and penalties. The ADs had regular 40-hour-a-week jobs at the station, and the hockey assignment was bonus money. The ADs' attitude about hockey ranged from intense interest to indifference. It was just another job for some of them, and the result was not much information. Jack Kelly worked with me for the better part of a season, and was just amazing at the job. I'll never understand why he wasn't permanently assigned to the position. Management never realized that a sharp AD would be a priceless ingredient to our telecast.

How to be a Sportscaster

I called Boston Bruins hockey games for 44 years, but during that period and before, I was able to announce virtually every sport. My experience included the New England Patriots; the Boston Lobsters (professional tennis); four years of NHL telecasts for CBS-TV; America's Cup for CBS radio; Boston College football, basketball and hockey; National Doubles Tennis; and much more.

A lot of people have written to ask—how do you become a sportscaster? The opportunity has widened with the advent of expanded radio stations, cable systems, and the internet. Radio still offers the best opportunity. If you are a student in high school or college, the chances are good that your school has a radio station. Seize the opportunity to broadcast the school's sports. If no station is available, buy a digital recorder, record game after game, and critique your work. Many sportscasters who wind up as sports anchors on newscasts have succeeded without any play-by-play background, but I think that it should be a basic experience for anyone.

Diligent practice with a recorder is a key to success. Many magazine advertisements make good copy, and the ability to read them in a professional manner, with the proper inflection, can enhance one's talent. The play-by-play announcer should be able to deliver a commercial effectively. A simple skill like being able to type is a must.

Needless to say, a good voice is essential and versatility can open many doors. Some candidates just concentrate on a sport that they like—it is not a good idea. Versatility is key. My first sports broadcast was tennis, and I was 28 years old at the time. World War II had delayed my entrance into the radio field.

Assuming that you have practiced diligently with your recorder, and that your evaluation of the game is reasonably professional, set up an appointment with a radio station or cable system manager. Discuss sports opportunities that the station is missing. I live in a market of 200,000 with about 17 radio stations, and a cable system of 70,000 subscribers. The high school football team in the largest town is not covered by a radio broadcast, even though it won the Division I title a few years ago. In approaching this market, I would point out to the radio station manager or cable system operator how coverage of this talented football team would not only enhance the broadcaster's image, but could bring in revenue.

A candidate should be willing to sell the broadcast or telecast as well as do the play-by-play—even if it is girls' volleyball. That's a sport that can be covered with one camera, videotaped, and presented at a later time. In 1980, I was concerned about the lack of coverage of the talented Barnstable High School hockey team on Cape Cod. Even though I had a busy schedule, I secured a camera, arranged for the rights fee, sold three sponsors, did the play-by-play, and packaged tape-delayed coverage of the team's bid for a state championship. They won—everybody was delighted. The key was selling the event, but that was the easiest part. Many people thought it was a TV38 production, even though we had only one camera.

I recall one year when WSBK-TV38 acquired the rights to televise the Red Sox. After the game they had a program called *Red Sox Re-Cap*. It was usually done by Tom Larson, but for some reason he passed it up. Although I lived on the Cape, and had an hour-and-a-half commute, I agreed to take the job. Unlike today's pre- and postgame shows, this one simply reported what occurred. No opinions were expressed regarding the quality of play. The program was designed to replay the highlights of the game just concluded. It was the toughest assignment I had in my radio and television career.

I operated out of the station's control room where the studio director of the baseball game worked. He inserted the commercials during the game. I sat at a typewriter and typed out a script that essentially introduced and exited highlights of the game—basically the runs scored. The game had to be followed in its entirety and fortunately, time was not of the essence. If the score ended 2–1 then obviously 15 minutes would be enough in the recap. If an exciting defensive play was made in the third inning, I had to decide whether to keep it or not. If the game turned out to be a low-scoring one, then obviously I should keep it for the highlights. A 9–8 score was something else. When the game ended, I had a couple of minutes to conclude the writing, give a copy to the director who would be winging it, and prepare to go before the camera with this unrehearsed program. There would be ample opportunity for gaffes, but I was able to get through the season without any major ones. A talented technical staff was most helpful. TV38 had a wonderful crew in the control room for every game. In essence, for this 15- or 20-minute program I was the producer, writer, and talent. One season was enough.

I was not much for hockey statistics. In some cities, the public relations director would swamp you with irrelevant stats. They usually weren't significant, and in hockey, you seldom had time to use them. One that I always thought was important, and kept tabs on, was shots on goal. They didn't always indicate a trend in the game, but I used them regularly. On March 22, 1991, the Bruins were playing Quebec and Ron Tugnutt was in goal for the Nordiques. As I watch the game in replay now, I did my usual job of indicating shots on net all through the game—not just when they became significant in the third period. For Tugnutt, they started to pile up. It turned out to be a night to remember as the Bruins unloaded 73 shots on him—three beat him, and the game wound up in a 3–3 tie. As I listen and watch hockey now, I want the announcer to keep pace with the shots on net.

What qualities are needed in a good sports announcer? A dedication to practice, versatility, a good voice, a willingness to take on any assignment, ad lib ability, play-by-play skill—these are the assets that can bring success in the sportscasting field.

When I was hired to be the analyst for the CBS TV *Hockey Game of the Week* in 1958, I was delighted with the opportunity. Peter Molnar was the producer, Joe Gallagher his assistant, and Chet Forte was an intern/gopher. Chet went on to fame and fortune as the director of *Monday Night Football* on ABC TV. The play-by-play announcer was Bud Palmer, who had been a basketball star at Princeton and was the announcer on WPIX TV, a New York independent station that covered Knicks and Rangers games. It soon became obvious to me that I was the most knowledgeable hockey person among the group, and my suggestions and recommendations were used.

The director, who was based in Chicago, was a character who was anxious to try anything new. The game coverage for the early afternoon telecast was pretty standard, but the innovations would come in the intermissions. Equipment was analyzed, and goaltenders did a lot of explaining of their roles. My memory of the director is that his pregame preparation consisted of downing a couple of shots of gin at Billy Goat's (named so because the proprietor resembled a billy goat with his goatee), a well-known bar located across the street from the Chicago Stadium. Considering it was still morning, I was somewhat taken aback, but it never affected his work. If he needed a refresher once the game began, the bars in Chicago Stadium were always open.

When they learned that I had been a hockey player at Northeastern University, they insisted that I do a feature on skates between periods. I would line up a player with a wireless mike, and we would demonstrate offside, icing, penalties, and any rules that were significant. The ratings for the games were highest in New England, but they were low around the country. CBS TV owned the station in St. Louis, but the general manager thought so little of hockey that he ran old movies instead.

After three years of coverage, the rating picture had not changed, but CBS authorized a fourth year in 1961. Bud Palmer had lined up other work on another network, so I was asked to do the play-by-play. We needed an analyst, and I suggested Brian McFarlane, who had been working in Schenectady, New York, in television. Although he was Canadian, he was a graduate of St. Lawrence University, where he had been a star hockey player. He was delighted to get the job. The first game was to be Detroit at New York on a Saturday afternoon. Our production and announcing crew were to meet in New York on Friday night; but when we got there, there was no sight of McFarlane. He had been stopped at the border in Windsor, Ontario, by Immigration Authorities. A protest had been lodged by the American Federation of Television and Radio Artists against CBS TV because they hired a non-American for the hockey position. AFTRA offered the names of 12 other hockey announcers (all Americans) as an alternative to McFarlane. Nothing could be done at this late hour, so management decided that I would do the game alone. Via split screen, I did interviews with players and Coach Muzz Patrick of New York in addition to handling the play-by-play. I was on for the entire three hours. On Monday, a meeting in the CBS headquarters was held to solve the problem. The network wanted no part of the 12 alternates, but how to keep McFarlane? Joe Gallagher made the suggestion that since Cusick did skating features between periods, his replacement would have to do the same. After a survey, AFTRA realized that none of the 12 recommended could skate and finally allowed McFarlane to be the analyst.

CBS dropped the games after the fourth year, but that season proved to be a launching pad for McFarlane's career. He returned to Canada for an assignment as intermission host on *Hockey Night in Canada*, the country's No. 1-rated program. He later served as commentator on NBC's hockey coverage, and in his spare time, he authored 50 books on hockey.

There is no question that good eyesight is a must for a hockey broadcaster. The puck is small, and the seating location in some cities is not adequate. When I started, identification was easy because no one wore helmets or facemasks. I had excellent vision until I hit my 50s, and then I was helped by glasses. My vision remained more than capable until my last year of NHL work in 1997. I had a detached retina that needed immediate attention, and Dr. Henry Krigstein performed the operation at Jordan Hospital in Plymouth, Massachusetts. I missed some games, and upon returning, I had a decided loss of vision in my left eye. I was able to finish the season, but I then retired.

Not as critical, but certainly very helpful, is good hearing. Unfortunately, hearing loss is an occupational hazard that afflicts many sportscasters. Wearing headphones simply directs the thunderous arena noise into your ears, and after years of wearing them, many broadcasters suffer hearing loss. I wear two hearing aides to help me overcome the problem. Pete Townshend, a longtime guitarist with the rock group, The Who, has also suffered hearing loss. He said his hearing problems are due to wearing headphones in the recording studio. Townshend has issued a warning to youngsters using iPod and MP3 headphones at high volumes—he says that they are headed for trouble. I concur—all the new technology is great, but headphones can do a lot of damage over time. Protect your hearing—it is too valuable to lose.

CHAPTER TWELVE

Broadcasting Other Sports

My job at WEEI, and my need to supplement my Bruins work led me to broadcast other sports throughout the years. After four years of televising National Hockey League games for CBS TV, I was hired by John Pinto, vice president of RKO General, to televise 25 regular-season games of the Boston Bruins and New York Rangers on Channel 17—an experimental pay-TV channel in Hartford, Connecticut. I did it for four years until RKO General abandoned the project. They spent about $12 million trying to make it work, but it was before its time in the early '60s. Since I was only doing 25 games during this schedule, I had time for other sports.

Football

I was present at the creation of the New England Patriots, and a difficult time it was. When the Boston Patriots (later the New England Patriots) made their debut in an exhibition game against the

Bills on July 30, 1960, at Buffalo War Memorial Stadium, I was there. My assignment was to handle the analysis. Bob Gallagher was the play-by-play man. WEEI had obtained the rights to broadcast the Patriots, along with the rights for Boston College football, which we had been doing for a couple of years. My policy was to announce as many Boston College games as I could, and to do the analysis on whatever Patriot games I was able to.

That first game in Buffalo quickly set the tone for the football team. It's hard to believe in these days when everybody connected with the NFL is drenched in money, but back then, the AFL Patriots were just scraping by. When they checked into a hotel, coach Lou Saban asked the team to take their afternoon naps on top of the beds and not disturb the sheets. If they did that, the team could obtain a special rate discount.

Things were so tight that the Patriots had trouble finding places to play. They could just as well have been known as The Gypsies. They played at Braves Field, Fenway Park, Harvard Stadium, and Boston College's Alumni Field. It was a "catch as catch can" activity. They used any vacant field that they could. One was located between the exit and entrance roads to Logan Airport. Shower facilities were at a minimum. In 1964, Fenway Park was not exactly user-friendly for football. The field ran from the third base line out to right field. Media used a couple of sky-view boxes overlooking the right field foul line.

Team owner Bill Sullivan desperately needed television coverage of a Friday night game. There was no chance of any network exposure, and the three local stations—4, 5, and 7—would not clear time. There were no independent stations. Sullivan approached me with the idea of having the television production company that I operated tape the game. The three hours of taping were to be condensed into an hour for replay on Channel 7 on Saturday morning. I would do the voice over. We agreed to a low-budget arrangement, and hired Channel 9's mobile unit from Manchester, New Hampshire. The pickup was to be done with one camera connected to a truck in the parking lot with a tape machine. Selling advertising time was an ordeal, because sponsors were not exactly standing in line.

Ultimately, we were able to get enough sponsors to put the program on. One of them was a national account, represented by a Boston advertising agency, Blackstone Cigars. They had one problem, though—all of their advertising had been in the print media, and they had no television commercials. We assured them that we would make one, and would get a Patriot player to do it. Nick Buoniconti, a Springfield native, who had been drafted by the Patriots after playing for Notre Dame, agreed to the project, even though we explained that he would have to do it before the game, in uniform, and up in the temporary press box. The fee was to be $100, and it would be paid by the agency.

Nick really got a pregame workout. He had to scramble up a couple of flights of stairs to the sky view box where our one camera was located, and read the message from some hastily prepared cue cards. Between the taping on Friday evening and the program on Saturday, the tape was lost. I still have in my possession a copy of a letter that Buoniconti sent to the advertising agency a month after the season ended requesting payment. He pointed out the great sacrifice that he made before the game, that he understood that he was to be paid whether the commercial ran or not; and he concluded that if he was not paid, he would turn the matter over to his attorney. The attorney could have been Nick himself, since he was already a lawyer.

Buoniconti went on to have a great career with the Miami Dolphins where, despite his size, he performed brilliantly. His legendary coach, Don Shula, said of him, "He's not tall enough to be a middle linebacker, but with his speed and intelligence, he is in the right place at the right time." Nick was 5-foot-11, and weighed 220 pounds. When the NFL and the AFL merged, he was chosen as the All-Time AFL middle linebacker. He was captain of the Dolphins, and led them to two Super Bowl titles in 1973 and 1974. The team was undefeated in the 1972 season. In all, he played seven seasons with the Miami Dolphins. A Buoniconti-style player today would command a salary of $10 or $12 million. That's a long way from his $100 pay for a commercial in his Patriot days.

Buoniconti has spent decades as co-host with Len Dawson of Home Box Office's *Inside the National Football League*. It is a weekly program, in season, offering a review and analysis of games along with predictions. Not too many sports personalities have lasted that long in television.

Baseball

My producing duties also led me to develop one of the first sports personality TV shows in Boston; it involved a ball player named Dick Stuart. There is nowadays a battle going on among Boston's Channels 4, 5, and 7 for supremacy in late Sunday night sports programs. Channels 4 and 7 feature 30-minute shows that highlight the hot sports topics of the day.

I put together the first of these shows in 1963, featuring Stuart, a newly acquired Red Sox first baseman. At the time, Channel 4 had a 15-minute newscast at 11 o'clock on Sunday night. I sold management on the idea of putting a 15-minute sports show at 11:15. Two sponsors jumped on board when I was able to produce Stuart as the host. The Sox had just secured him in a trade with Pittsburgh, and I had reports that he was not only a powerful home-run hitter, but also a colorful character off the field. He agreed to do the program for a fee of $150 per show. No agents were involved, and the Red Sox, whose fortunes were in the doldrums, were delighted with the publicity.

The program was to highlight Stuart live each Sunday night. When the Sox were on the road, he would be featured in prerecorded interviews. Gene Pell, a newscaster, would be on hand to introduce Stuart and his guest, and handle the scores and other news. Stuart was no Jack Paar or Johnny Carson, but he was an impeccably dressed tall and handsome figure in addition to owning an impressive slugging record. In five years with Pittsburgh, he had hit 117 home runs, including one that went out of Forbes Field and landed 500 feet from home plate—the longest ever hit there. He's the only ball player to hit over 200 homers in both his minor and major league careers.

To say the least, the first few programs were not smooth. Stuart felt that since the show bore his name, he had to do the talking. His guest introductions and his questions were much too long. The dialogue at times sounded like a Bob-and-Ray skit, the one where the interviewer constantly repeats the answers of the interviewee. Sometimes people laughed at Stuart, and sometimes they laughed with him, but they were still watching and talking about the program.

As a hitter, Dick Stuart was made for Fenway Park. That first season he hit 42 home runs and drove in 118; but sometimes his fielding was not up to par. He didn't make many errors, but when he did, they were at the most inopportune times. Somebody tagged him with the name "Dr. Strange Glove" from the Peter Sellers movie that was in vogue at the time. Dick took the moniker in stride, and it was fortunate for his critics that he did. Reports were that he was the peacekeeper in the clubhouse. He was as talented in fighting as he was as a hitter. One of his other talents was arm wrestling. Stuart claimed he never lost a match.

For all his slugging ability, Stuart fanned a lot; he was the team leader in strikeouts. But he had a sense of humor. On one program, I had Bud Collins, now the esteemed tennis columnist for *The Boston Globe*, but then a sports reporter for *The Boston Herald*, appear to present Stuart an award. Dick had no idea what it was for. The trophy showed a crouched hockey player lining up for a face-off. Collins presented the trophy in reverse and called it "the Fanny Award." Stuart laughed as hard as anybody.

The program attracted what could best be called a lot of notoriety. *Sports Illustrated* did a column on it and the ratings were good. By far, the most memorable show was the night that Stuart invited his manager, Johnny Pesky. The former Red Sox shortstop was in his first year at the helm. His playing record was superb. A lifetime .307 hitter, he, along with Dom DiMaggio, had proven to be the ideal set-up man for Ted Williams.

If you are introducing your boss, it is generally not a good idea to point out his faults. Pesky had been part of a memorable moment in Red Sox history. Naturally it had negative implications. In Game 7 of the 1946 World Series against the St. Louis Cardinals, the score was tied 3–3 in the eighth. Enos Slaughter singled, then broke for second as Harry Walker lined the ball to right center for a hit. Slaughter never stopped running as the relay came to Pesky, who threw to the plate too late to catch the speedy runner. Was Slaughter the hero, and Pesky the goat? The controversy has lingered through the years.

To my amazement, that Sunday night, Dick Stuart's introduction of the manager included details of the one play that Pesky would like to forget. He had to be stunned, but Pesky handled it well. Their relationship after that had to be on the cool side, but Stuart was oblivious to how his manager felt. The program was cancelled after 26 weeks—although the sponsors wanted to continue. The director who handled the preceding 11 o'clock news had to direct the "imported" sports program at no extra pay. His negative comments to management brought about the cancellation. Stuart stayed with the team for another season.

Pesky, of course, has been a longtime organization man, working in community relations currently. When the Red Sox initiated a Hall of Fame in 1995, Pesky was among the first inductees. Stuart was not inducted even though in a two-year span he hit 75 home runs and batted in 224 runs.

In the '60s, I had a pretty good connection to baseball. To begin with, Dick O'Connell, who became the general manager of the Red Sox, was in my Naval Reserve unit. Occasionally, he would schedule a meeting at Fenway Park. It consisted of dinner in the press room and a discussion of the projects that the public relations unit was working on. The members would then watch the game. I was a regular member of the press corps, and in that capacity, I was pretty much a frequent visitor. I had established a program feature on WEEI that formed a close connection with the Red Sox. The Hotel Kenmore had an elegant dining facility called the "Clubhouse Restaurant."

I conducted a Monday-through-Friday interview program on WEEI at 6:15 each evening. I would highlight the sports news of the day, and spend the rest of the 15-minute program on the interview. The guests ranged far and wide over the sports world, but because of its location, there was an emphasis on baseball and its personnel. Talent fee? How about a delicious dinner from soup to nuts? I would usually join the guest and enjoy a meal after the broadcast. Some guests brought their wives and they were welcomed. The guest was also given a gift certificate from Webb's Men's Store, located 50 yards from the Hotel Kenmore. I had no trouble getting guests. After a rare day game, a visiting broadcaster—such as Ernie Harwell of Detroit—was delighted to join. The Hotel Kenmore usually hosted the visiting teams.

My closest connection to baseball was when I spent two years as the public address announcer for the Red Sox. I had a busy winter schedule, but I was happy with more to do in the summer. Money was not the issue—it was about having something more to do than just play golf. The Red Sox pay was just $12 per game. My wife and I had just joined the Woodland Golf Club in Newton, just outside of Boston. We lived in Newton Lower Falls, just up the street from the seventh hole of the Club. I was an indifferent golfer, but the Club had a swimming pool that my children loved. My wife turned into a terrific golfer and won the Ladies championship twice. Obviously, my Red Sox endeavors would not help to pay much of my golf expenses. I also learned that in addition to announcing, I was to run the scoreboard—every ball, every strike, every out—by flicking a switch in front of me. I would put on a light on the scoreboard that would indicate the significant number. It meant total concentration for the entire game.

Until 1967 when they won the pennant, the Red Sox did not draw all that many fans. Media coverage was not great, and the Boston papers sent Bud Collins of the *Herald*, Larry Claflin of the *American*, Clif Keane of the *Globe*, and Bill Liston of the *Traveler*. They would huddle behind my public address area and talk about a variety of subjects. When the wind turned, bringing the cold breeze from the East, they would go into the press room, order up a beer and keep track of the game via radio or television. I did not have that luxury available. I always brought warm clothing to prepare for the wind change, but it never seemed adequate. The caliber of baseball was not that great. For instance, a doubleheader between the Red Sox and the White Sox might result in scores of 13–9 or 8–6. That meant over seven hours of baseball plus an intermission, which made for a long day of watching and recording every pitch. Since it was the White Sox, I would reflect on the job that Bob Elson had. He was the Chicago announcer on radio. He had to follow this team every day. His remuneration was a lot more than mine, but he earned it.

Whenever the White Sox came to town, Elson would have me on his pregame show. In the winter he was the voice of the Chicago Blackhawks. Oddly enough, I returned for a second year despite the fact that there was no increase in salary. Two years were enough, though, and my successor was the golden-voiced Vin Maloney. Vin was in the Navy unit, so Dick O'Connell had no problem naming him. After Vin, the voice was Sherm Feller. He made it a state-of-the-art job by adding a simple phrase to his game introduction. I would say: "Good afternoon, ladies and gentlemen." Sherm simply added:

"Boys and girls." The team got better and won the pennant in 1967 under Dick Williams.

Joe DiMaggio

One of the bonuses of doing radio and/or television coverage of the Bruins was traveling with a compatible group of newspapermen, who made life on the road enjoyable. For the Boston papers, there was a regular group–Tom Fitzgerald and Herb Ralby of the *Globe*, Henry McKenna of the *Herald*, Leo Monahan of the *Record*, Bill Liston and Nick Del Ninno of the *Traveler*, and Roger Barry of the *Patriot Ledger*. Bill Grimes of the *American* didn't travel, but wrote his stories off the radio broadcast. Ralby and Barry were in the conflicting role of being Bruins publicists as well as reporters. They carried it off well, and no one complained. Of the group, Tom Fitzgerald was the most entertaining. He was a natural-born storyteller, and if he was the butt of the joke—so much the better.

Fitzie's best story concerned Joe DiMaggio. Fitzie had returned from Army service, and resumed his job writing for the *Globe* sports pages with particular emphasis on hockey and golf. In 1946, the Red Sox turned in a terrific season. They had captured the American league pennant and were preparing to face the St. Louis Cardinals. The *Globe* went all out in its coverage; and when the games were in St. Louis, Jerry Nason, the sports editor, led the parade of writers on the road. Tom Fitzgerald was left at home as the acting editor.

Jack Hamilton, an advertising salesman for the *Globe*, was also a big sports fan. His coverage for ads included the Hub's Rialto and nightclubs. One night, he visited the club at the Hotel Touraine on Boylston Street. He watched, and later chatted, with a featured performer who played the accordion and sang. Her name was Bea Sharpe. Noticing a huge engagement ring on her hand, Jack asked whom the lucky man might be. "Joe DiMaggio," she responded, and then discreetly detailed plans for the marriage. Hamilton's head started spinning, and the words "stop the presses" kept ringing in his ears.

An all-encompassing story on DiMaggio had recently appeared in the *Globe*. It had pointed out that in 1946, after Army service, the Yankee Clipper was not exactly a recluse. The nightlife of New York fascinated him, and having been divorced from Dorothy Arnold, he had a penchant for showgirls. It was not unusual for him to show up at Toots Shor's celebrity-filled restaurant with a beautiful girl on his arm.

Hamilton cabbed it back to the *Globe's* sports department, and there imparted the priceless news to the man in charge—Tom Fitzgerald. Fitzie was as excited as Hamilton, and decided to cover the story himself. He was soon at the Touraine interviewing Bea Sharpe to confirm Hamilton's report. Getting as many details as he could, he went back to the *Globe*. He cleared away the routine World Series stories, and placed the rarely seen "Copyright *Boston Globe*" on his exclusive. It ran on the front page. When DiMaggio was contacted, he was furious that his privacy had been invaded. He denied the story, and had a few well-chosen words to describe his opinion of Fitzgerald. Fortunately for Fitzie, he never had to cover baseball and so he never met DiMaggio face to face. But the story doesn't end there. Boston's own Gillette Razor Company sponsored a jingle that got universal coverage in sports programs. Its opening lines, sung by a quartet were:

"To look sharp and be on the ball."

"To be sharp and you'll get the call…"

For quite a while after that, Tom Fitzgerald was greeted by his colleagues with the Gillette jingle wherever he went.

Tennis

Another sport that I dabbled in was tennis. The World Team Tennis League was formed in 1974, and the Boston entry, owned by Bob Kraft, was known as the Lobsters. Playing a countrywide schedule of 44 matches and featuring some of the biggest names in the sport, I thought it could be a viable operation. Bob Kraft brought the same first-class operation to the endeavor as he did later with the New England Patriots. His star attraction was Martina Navratilova. Other teams featured names like Billie Jean King in New York, Chris Evert in Los Angeles, Virginia Wade in San Francisco, Cliff Drysdale in Anaheim, Jimmy Connors in Baltimore, and Rod Laver in San Diego. Those players got big money, but with such a tremendous overhead, the League was doomed. It has somehow survived, but with a much lower budget.

The Lobsters played their home matches at the Walter Brown Arena. Bud Collins of *The Boston Globe* and Channel 2 did the tennis coverage of selected matches on Channel 38. I did the backup, and when Bud could not make the event because of a conflict, I did the hosting.

Wrestling

Wrestling was a pretty popular sport in the 1930s. Paul Bowser was *THE* promoter in Boston and New England. He ran shows in the Boston Arena, and when it was a big "championship" event, he staged it at the Boston Garden. One of his assistants was a Waltham, Massachusetts, native Eddie Quinn. Eddie began staging small events in Waltham, and heard of an opportunity to be a promoter in Montreal. The sport had not been faring well in Canada, but with a showman's flare, Quinn revived it. His meal ticket was Yvon Robert, who became as famous as a wrestler (particularly in the province of Quebec) as Rocket Richard was in hockey. Quinn made wrestling a million-dollar industry in Canada, and it was second in popularity to hockey. He branched out and became a nightclub owner by buying the famous El Morroco, located across the street from the Forum. In 1957, the Bruins were in the playoffs against the Montreal Canadiens, and that meant a press room suite in the Sheraton Hotel would operate for several days and nights. As a native of greater Boston, Eddie Quinn was a regular visitor, and would regale the writers and others in attendance with stories about the wrestling business in Canada. He earned everlasting gratitude from the Boston media when he invited all of them to dinner and a show at El Morroco. That night, he must have picked up a substantial tab, but Eddie was a big spender and he didn't blink.

When Eddie Quinn was breaking into the wrestling business in the '30s, Paul Bowser had a wide variety of performers led by Gus Sonnenberg and Danno Mahoney, who ranked at various times as "champions." Fred Bruno was a journeyman who traveled the circuit. When he retired, Bowser set him up as a promoter. When I got my first job in broadcasting on Cape Cod in 1946, Bruno was staging weekly summertime events at the Mill Hill Arena in West Yarmouth; only it wasn't an arena—it was an open field with a ring and portable chairs that could seat about 800 fans. Each week, Bruno would come down the night before a show, visit the media to promote it, and pray that there was no rain in the weather forecast. I would have lunch with him the day of the event.

I was also employed as a ticket taker. Since I was making $32 a week, the lunch and the job helped out my bottom line. His star performer, who was always in the final match of the evening, was Ted Germaine. He was sort of a "champion" in the hinterlands outside of Boston. The wrestlers all arrived at about the same time in a couple of limousines. One night, they were short one performer, who was to meet a young local lad making his debut. Without hesitation, Fred Bruno stepped into the breech, figuring his experience would be an equalizer. It was one of the most gripping wrestling matches I have ever seen. There was nothing staged in it. The young man wanted to prove his worth, and 55-year-old Fred Bruno had all he could handle. They called it a draw after 20 minutes.

The famous Vince McMahon, impresario of the World Wrestling Federation, passed through Cape Cod for a couple of years, but it was a case of "Vince, we hardly knew ye." He bought the Cape Cod Coliseum, which was built at the height of hockey mania, and housed the Cape Cod Cubs of the Eastern Hockey League, high school hockey, and various other events. While Vince owned the building, he was anything but flamboyant, and his quiet directorship meant the end of the arena. It was turned into a warehouse.

Boxing

I've had a lot of ideas for sports television, and some of them worked. One that didn't was *Search for a Champion*, which I still consider a very viable idea. In 1982, I acted on a concept and put together a pilot program with my own money. My theory was that boxing was widely appealing, but not comprehended. People watched it without understanding the skill and science that champion boxers had to have. Why not a show that would demonstrate that talent with a former champion doing the commentary? Paul Pender proved to be the ideal candidate. In 1948, when I was broadcasting Brookline High football games, he was an outstanding end on the team. He had taken up boxing and shown great skill despite a pair of brittle hands. In a 48-bout career, he had won 40 fights—20 of them by knockouts.

On January 22, 1960, he won the world middleweight title with a 15-round split decision over Sugar Ray Robinson at Boston Garden. Sugar Ray was past his prime and didn't have speed anymore. In his younger days, he had been regarded as the best fighter of all time. Regardless, Pender was the winner and champion and repeated the feat later. He retired as a champion in 1963.

Pender had attended Emerson College, and was one of the most articulate boxers in the game. I felt that he would be a natural as the analyst. He agreed to do a pilot program for $150. My other cost was a cameraman and a camera. The boxer we were to examine critically would not have to be paid. As a matter of fact, he should pay us for the top-of-the-line critique that would result. We went to an amateur fight show in Dartmouth, Massachusetts; received permission for a close-up camera location, and asked who was the best fighter to perform that night. There was unanimous agreement that it was Vinny Pazienza. We taped his fight with incisive commentary by Pender, and later did an interview in which Paul told Vinny what he had to do to become a champion. Bright and eager to learn, Vinny followed the advice to become the world lightweight champion in1987. Later, he put on about 24 pounds to win the world junior middleweight championship. The edited program developed into an instructive and entertaining half-hour, but I could not get it on the air—even on cable. It is still viable, and Pazienza would be the ideal candidate.

College Football

I played football at St. Columbkille's High School in Brighton, and at Northeastern University, but I can't say that I ever enjoyed it. I only played it to better prepare myself for hockey. Now there was sport that was enjoyable to practice and play! In football, I was a guard and went out for the freshman team at Northeastern. Oddly enough, they practiced at their Kent Street Field in Brookline, Massachusetts, at noontime. The varsity coach was Jimmy Dunn, and his assistants were Harold Kopp, Jerry Tatton, and Herb Gallagher. Dunn and Kopp had played college football under Dick Harlow at Western Maryland (now McDaniel College), and later served as assistant coaches at Harvard under Harlow. Harlow had established a national reputation as a coach by developing an offense that was based on deception and timing. Naturally, Dunn and Kopp brought the system to Northeastern. In no way did it match the formations that coaches use today at all levels—high school, college, and professional.

The quarterback is the key today, while in the Harlow system, the fullback was the important backfield player. Basically, it was a single-wing system; a tailback lined up directly behind center, four yards back. To his right was the fullback, a yard ahead. The quarterback, whose primary duty was blocking, lined up behind the right tackle, and a wingback lined up outside the right end. Most of the time, the ball was snapped to the fullback. He was a "spinner" who turned and gave the ball to the tailback, who was generally led by the two guards on a run to the right. Sometimes the fullback kept the ball after faking it to the tailback, and gave it to the wingback, who was coming back on a reverse. In the mid-'30s, Harlow had a fullback at Harvard, Vernon Struck, who was just about perfect in the role. He was called the "magnificent faker."

Our freshman team at Northeastern never quite adapted to the system, and we never won a game. When I started as a member of the squad, I ranked third or fourth on the list of guards. At the end of the season, I was starting—not because of talent, but because for one reason or another, students had dropped out of school. As a guard, it was my duty to lead the attack, but my lack of speed hampered me. I played one year on the varsity squad but never enjoyed the practice time, and I seldom even got into a game.

There is certainly no requisite that a broadcaster should have played the game he is covering, but it helps. I know of several hockey play-by-play men who never laced up a pair of skates. My brief football experience helped me when I started at WBET in Brockton, Massachusetts, covering the local high school team. Later at WEEI, I managed to squeeze in quite a few Boston College football games, especially at the start of the season. Many of the Boston College alumni loved the sport. They backed it enthusiastically, and each season revived their hopes that the team would make it to a bowl game as they had under Frank Leahy.

In 1962, the team opened with a win over the University of Cincinnati 25–0. A key test, though, would be their second game against Northwestern in Chicago. Many of the alumni booked air flights the following week to cheer on the team. I was on the charter flight with the team. As the team spread out over the field, the Northwestern coach, Ara Parseghian showed up. This was *THE* Ara

Parseghian who went on to great fame as the coach of Notre Dame. The Boston press, eager to get his opinion of the Eagles team, surrounded him.

"Wow," Parseghian said, "just look at the size of that team—they're monsters—look at the field, it's tilting."

Boston was a big team, but their problem was a lack of speed. After three minutes of play on Saturday afternoon, Boston College was behind 14–0 and Northwestern went on to crush them. It was a tough game for me to broadcast, but it was tougher on the loyal alumni who had made the trek to Chicago.

When Channel 56 lost the Bruins, I was able to set up some freelance work in radio. Ted Peene, who owned radio station WTTT in Amherst, had acquired the rights to University of Massachusetts football. I signed on as the play-by-play man, and had many an enjoyable Saturday afternoon covering the team. Broadcasters have found that winning makes the job easier, and with Vic Fusia as head coach and Greg Landry as quarterback, UMass usually won. Landry went on to a splendid career in pro football with the Detroit Lions.

Politics and Clothes

One of my oddest broadcasting experiences during those years had nothing to do with sports; it was all about politics. Well, politics and clothes.

I was about the third person hired at WKBG, Channel 56, in 1967. They had rights to the Bruins telecasts for one year, and Weston Adams, president of the team, made it clear that I was part of the deal and would announce the games. However, I felt I could offer more to the station. I had a background producing a variety of shows, plus I was local. But first, Jim Lynagh, the new general manager, had to get a studio location.

Lynagh summoned the forces of Kaiser Industries, which owned the station. About 10 young executives, most of them with MBAs, came to Boston to scour the area for a suitable place. I attended their meetings and was duly impressed with their detailed analysis of the problem and how they would attack it. After much deliberation they settled on 1050 Commonwealth Avenue, second floor. In a month, the studios and offices were set up; and as soon as the tower was ready, Channel 56 would be in business. While waiting, it was decided to offer the place for rent to outside agencies for production purposes.

First to take advantage of this was the campaign of Senator Eugene McCarthy, running for president of the United States. He was running in New Hampshire, and wanted to tape a 15-minute program for viewing in that state. He had a scoop of sorts. He would be introduced by the recently retired Jack Paar, longtime host of *The Tonight Show* on NBC.

WKBG provided a set with a desk and books in the backdrop. Paar was to sit on the edge of the desk for the intro, and McCarthy would be sitting in a comfortable chair behind the desk. No teleprompter was needed.

When everything was ready, the director gave the cue, and the assistant director pointed to Paar. Jack smiled and said, "Hello, I'm Jack Paar, here to introduce…"

His voice broke off, for just then a tremendous roar like the sound of an express train in a tunnel came up from the floor. A startled Paar said, "What the hell is that?" Everything stopped and a search was made. Ultimately it was discovered that the first-floor tenant was a wholesale dress distributor, who had a large array of racks with dresses on them. When shipments had to be made, the dresses were rolled out on the racks, and a sound as loud as thunder exploded. A truce was arranged. The dress man would notify WKBG when the racks were going to roll. The Channel 56 production crew had to work around that schedule until a new site was found. Paar and McCarthy completed their assignment that day. It was too bad that Paar had retired from NBC. I think the dress rack episode could have found a place in one of his monologues. I have often thought of the 10 MBAs who picked the studio site. For all of their education, they could not have picked a worse spot.

CHAPTER THIRTEEN

Fore!

From Caddy to Champion

In 1963, The Country Club in Brookline honored Francis Ouimet by hosting the U.S. Open. Fifty years before, Ouimet had won the Open at The Country Club as a 20-year-old caddy. He defeated Harry Vardon and Ted Ray, two world-famous golfers from Great Britain. That year, I was sports director of WEEI radio. I took note of the fact that the four Boston television stations were not doing much with Ouimet or covering the tournament. I thought that an interview with him would be a good idea.

I approached him with the idea of doing an interview on Channel 2, Boston's public station. He was agreeable, and I talked to Channel 2 people about doing a Q&A at the station. They had a new mobile unit with a wireless mike and were anxious to try it out, so they suggested we do it at The Country Club. I sketched out a format that included doing about 15 minutes discussing the clubs and balls used in 1913, talking about the Ouimet Caddy Fund, and showing the famous picture of Ouimet when he was inducted as the first American captain of the Royal and Ancient Golf Club of St. Andrews. The second part of the 30-minute interview would employ the wireless microphones as we walked out of the clubhouse and towards the 17th green, as Ouimet recapped his victory march in 1913. We did the entire program in one take, and were paid a dollar each.

Prior to the interview, I made a valiant attempt to be assigned as a reporter on the telecast by NBC. I had done four years of hockey coverage on CBS TV, and Craig Smith was a producer at that network. He had since moved to NBC TV, and was in charge of the U.S. Open telecast. At that time, ex-pros were not doing golf telecasts. Smith hired Bud Palmer and Chick Hearn, announcer types, to do the telecast. I was not selected, even though my Ouimet interview would have been a valuable addition. NBC TV's coverage began on the 14th hole, but a delay required them to fill an hour before the competitors arrived in camera range.

Unbelievably, my interview with Ouimet is the only one in existence today. For several years, it has been used by various TV and film companies in association with Channel 2. The United States Golf Association used it in an all-encompassing history of golf. The Ouimet Caddy Fund has used a portion in a fund-raising drive. The World Golf Hall of Fame in St. Augustine, Florida, also used a portion. Little did I expect that the interview would be considered "spellbinding," "vintage," and "cool" more than 40 years later by a whole new generation of sports fans.

In 2004, Disney made *The Greatest Game Ever Played*—a retelling of Ouimet's victory, based on the book by Mark Frost. Frost established a name for himself as a television writer/producer of *Twin*

Peaks and *Hill Street Blues.* As a golfer, he became interested in Francis Ouimet when Justin Leonard sank a 45-foot putt on the 17th hole at The Country Club in 1999 to win the Ryder Cup for the United States. A couple of birdies on the 17th hole had been pivotal to the success of Ouimet in the 1913 Open tournament. Frost did some research and came up with a beautifully written book, *The Greatest Game Ever Played.* He also wrote the screenplay of the Walt Disney movie with the same name.

My daughter-in-law, Laurie, suggested that I contact Disney to see if they would be interested in using a clip as a special feature for the DVD release. While the movie was successful at the box office, some reviewers of the DVD claimed that my interview was "the coolest part." Disney ended up using all 28 minutes of the broadcast. It's great to be part of the new technology.

Here, in part, is the Ouimet interview as we walked toward the 17th hole:

Cusick: How was your play as you moved along...let's say first round, second round...were you satisfied with your play?

Ouimet: Well, I was quite satisfied. I remember topping my tee shot on the first hole, and taking a six on the comparatively short second hole; and after that I got squared away and finished with a 74, which was extremely satisfying to me.

C: Of course all the talk, I suppose, was about Vardon and Ray and their great potentialities and their great play.

O: Oh yes, all together. Everybody was keen to see Vardon and Ray. They were regarded as the two best in the world, and of course we all wanted to see how well the American professionals would do, and particularly the imported English and Scotch pros...Vardon was a beautiful player—he had a picture-perfect swing, beautifully balanced. Ray was a huge man and a rather awkward player, but a very effective one.

C: Now you moved around first, second, third—when did you feel that you really had a shot at this Open championship?

O: Fred, I never really had a shot to win it, but I kept poking along and staying reasonably close to the leaders; and then it gets in your blood, and you feel you've got to keep going. While you don't think you're going to win the championship, you do feel that you are going to put together some good holes, make a good round, and let the round stand up, good or bad.

C: Moving along to the third round—and the fourth in particular—as you started out that day. What was the situation? Ray had already finished hadn't he?

O: Yes. It's a funny thing, as I was walking down to play my round, Ray was holing out on the 18th green right in front of me. We had tied at the three-quarter mark with scores of 225, and he had a 79 for that final round which gave him a 72-hole score of 304—so I knew exactly what I had to do.

C: That was the target there, and later Vardon came in and posted a 304; yet you started off a little rough in the first nine in the fourth round?

O: Oh yes, I fell to pieces in the middle of the nine and struggled out in 43 strokes.

C: Then how about the tenth hole—did you have trouble there too?

O: That was a nightmare. I hit my tee shot off that tenth tee about 20 feet and made a good recovery shot to the green, but ended up taking three putts for a five.

C: Well then it came down more or less, as you tell the story, Mr. Ouimet, to the 13th hole. You knew the situation—you knew the course that was in front of you if you wanted to at least tie for this Open championship. Is that right?

O: Yes. I knew that somewhere along the line on the last six holes—I didn't know where they had to come—I had to have four pars and two birdies, two holes under par. I didn't know which one; I was hoping it would be the first one I was playing.

C: Now the 13th, what did you do there?

O: Well, I didn't play what you would call a very good second shot, but I chipped in from the edge of the green, which gave me one of the very desirable birdies. I had a three there.

C: So you got one of your strokes there.

O: I got one of the strokes I was looking for. Fourteenth was uneventful. Fifteen was another exciting affair. I missed my second shot so badly it passed to the right of the trap, but I recovered nicely within a foot of the hole so I got my par four there.

C: Fine. Sixteenth—you might have counted on that as a possibility?

O: I was sort of hoping, all along, that I might pick up two on that hole. It was not a difficult par three, and I had been playing it well, and I had not had a two. I thought that perhaps I might get a two. You might say that it was a wish more than anything else. As a matter of fact, I had to hole a nine-foot putt for a three.

C: Oh, what a disappointment.

O: Yes it was.

C: At least you got your three and were still within range.

O: I got my three and still had a chance to get a birdie on the last two holes.

C: And we're coming to one now, and that's the 17th. I'm sure you would want to point out that it is not exactly the same as you played it, Mr. Ouimet.

O: That is right. The whole green was located to the left of that mound—in that general direction and it was a slanting green—it ran from right to left you see; it was protected by a trap in front and some mounds on the right. I got my second shot on the green in good position—maybe 15 feet from the hole—and I was lucky enough to hole that putt for the three that I needed so badly.

C: Well that was your birdie, and certainly a lot of cheers would have gone up.

O: Well, they said that there was quite a commotion caused by cars on the street, but I was concentrating so seriously that I didn't hear anything.

C: I can well imagine. You still, of course, had to play the 18th and get your four to stay within contention.

O: Yes, I needed a four to tie.

C: And that was fairly uneventful, or how did you feel about it?

O: Well, it was not altogether uneventful. I thought I hit a great second shot there; but when I got up to the ball, I found that it hit the top of the mound, and instead of kicking forward, it stopped right there. I finally had to chip within three feet of the hole and was lucky enough to make the putt.

C We might comment that your caddy at that time was 10 years old—Eddie Lowery.

O: Oh yes. Eddie Lowery—he was 10 years old.

C: How many clubs did he have to carry for you?

O: He had to carry 10—I probably used seven…the outside eight.

C: That's amazing…you tied.

O: That gave me 304 for 72 holes, and tied me with Vardon and Ray.

C: Of course, your work was not done; you had the proud privilege at age 20 of competing against these two top-flight professionals in a playoff.

O: That's right.

C: What about the playoff? What was the weather like and how did it go?

O: Well, the weather was very humid—it was misty and we carried umbrellas the early part of the match. The mist died away, but it was one of those sultry, heavy, soggy days.

C: As you moved along, there were opportunities for a young Mr. Ouimet to blow up, but you didn't. Finally, it was Mr. Ray, who sort of blew up on the 15th and moved out of contention.

O: Yes, it was anybody's match for 13 holes. At the end of 13 holes, I was leading by one stroke. Vardon came next—he was a stroke away from me, and Ray was two strokes away. Anything could have happened on those last five holes. On the 15th, Ray sliced his tee shot into the rough, put his second into a trap, took two to get out, and took a six on the hole to our fours. So that put him four behind me, three behind Vardon, and practically out of the running.

C: And then it was you and Mr. Vardon.

O: Practically speaking.

C: Again, the 17th was pivotal—right here as we stand on it.

O: It was a pivotal hole for sure.

C: What happened there?

O: Well, Vardon had the honor by virtue of having a three on the 13th, and since the other holes were halved, he still retained the honor playing the 17th hole. He hit a ball to the left, dangerously close to a trap. I couldn't tell whether it was in the trap or not, but I didn't want to take that line. So I hit my ball where I had driven it the day before—well to the right—to the right-hand side of the fairway.

When we got to our balls—his ball was in the trap which is known ever since as the Vardon trap. That trap was a very difficult trap to play out of. It sloped into a bank, and he was left with a downhill lie, from which it was impossible to play a normal recovery shot to the green. He had to play out to one side. In the meantime, I put my second shot on the green in two, and he got on in three. I had quite an edge there, particularly when a 15- or 18-foot putt dribbled into the hole for a three.

C: Remarkable, of course. Again, it was the 17th hole—two birdies on two successive days.

O: Yes, it was quite a coincidence that it happened to be that same hole on two successive days.

C: And so the 18th—you can't say that it was routine, but more or less it, must have been; and so you came through with the championship in this head-to-head match with Ray and Vardon. Twenty years old and a U.S. Open champion—that was a very historic victory for you, Francis Ouimet.

O: Well, it was one of those things that came out of the blue; I didn't expect to do it.

Francis Ouimet's 1913 victory in the U.S. Open changed his life. He became a successful stockbroker, and played in tournaments around the world. He won the National Amateur twice, and the Massachusetts Amateur six times; he either played on or captained the U.S. Walker Cup—the biennial amateur competition between America and Britain—team 10 times.

His proudest honor occurred in 1949, when the Francis Ouimet Caddy Scholarship Fund was created. It has grown to a multimillion-dollar endowment perpetuating the name of the man who brought golf to the masses, and college scholarships to its young players.

Golf reveals the true nature of its participants, and no one has been a better example than Francis Ouimet. Despite an early spotlight on his memorable triumph, he remained a humble, reticent, but congenial sportsman who loved the game of golf and everything associated with it. What Palmer, Nicklaus, Woods, and others have done to expand the appeal of the sport, Ouimet did in one week's spectacular play. He is golf's Man of the 20th Century.

It was fitting that a New England native, Julius Boros, should win the 1963 Open that commemorated Ouimet's victory. A native of Fairfield, Connecticut, Boros had not turned pro until he was 29 years old. Boros was overweight and looked like a weekend golfer, but he never played like one. He had a picture-perfect swing, and liked to play at an up-tempo pace. "Step up and hit the ball" was his motto. He never dawdled over putts. When he finished four rounds of play in 1963, he was nine over par and never figured he would be in a playoff, but the wind raised havoc with the finishers and Boros wound up in a tie with Jackie Cupit and Arnold Palmer. He beat them in a playoff.

Fred Corcoran

After my four years of doing the *Hockey Game of the Week* for CBS TV, I received a call from Fred Corcoran to have lunch with him at Toot Shors in New York. He had been named as a consultant to the National Hockey League, to secure another TV contract, but more importantly, to analyze the game and to offer ideas as to how it could be made more popular. He had made great strides in golf—a sport similar to hockey in that neither was easy to televise. As I prepared to meet him, I reflected on his fascinating background.

He was the visionary who saw golf as we know it today. His story is well told in a book—now out of print—*Unplayable Lies*. The autobiography, written with Bud Harvey, refers to Corcoran as an impresario. That's a much too pretentious word. Promoter and manager would suffice.

His roots were firmly planted in New England, but golf took him around the world. One of six sons of an itinerant worker in Cambridge, Massachusetts, Corcoran led a hand-to-mouth existence growing up. At the tender age of nine, he began work as a caddy at Belmont Springs, a course he could walk to from his home, which was then in Arlington, Massachusetts. It was shortly after Frances Ouimet had brought golf into the limelight.

Corcoran's tendency was to look at golf as a business. He was interested in the golf course setup, equipment, the day-to-day operation, and most of all, the people connected to the game. At the age of 12 he was the caddiemaster, and his management instinct was to get hands-on experience. He tried various jobs outside of golf, and until the age of 20, he was Massachusetts' golf handicapper. Fred's first contribution to the game was the scoreboard. He covered national and local tournaments, and introduced colored crayons to record birdies, pars, and bogies.

Wintertime service was spent in Pinehurst, North Carolina, as an assistant secretary to the legendary golf architect Donald Ross. Later, he became Secretary of the Massachusetts Golf Association, and in

1937 he became tournament manager of the PGA. In the winter, he served as ticket sales manager of the Boston Bruins for several years.

With the PGA, Corcoran entered a minefield of cliques, divided loyalties, and a not-too-happy array of sponsors. In his second tournament in Oakland, California, he hit the jackpot. The winner was a rangy, colorful player from Virginia, Sam Snead. Corcoran, who was a natural at public relations, cultivated the press with a myriad of stories about "Slammin' Sam." Corcoran became Snead's manager, and together, their fortunes grew as Snead became one of the top players in the game. Corcoran garnered endorsements and exhibition fees that delighted the frugal Snead. Although Corcoran had never worked on a newspaper, he knew what journalists wanted—a good story. A good press for golf, for the PGA, and for the players he represented, meant higher purses for the tour.

Snead brought others into the fold of Corcoran's successful managing. They included Tony Lema, Ken Venturi, and Bobby Nichols; and in baseball, Ted Williams and Stan Musial. He was vice-president of the International Canada Cup competition, and consultant to Shell's *Wonderful World of Golf* television program.

He organized the LPGA in 1948, and originated both the PGA and LPGA Halls of Fame. Corcoran was manager of the 1937 and 1953 Ryder Cup teams. He saw television in golf's future; and at one time, individually, held the television rights to the PGA Tour.

Golf opened doors in every direction for Fred Corcoran. He dealt with industry leaders who became sponsors. He was close to the Hollywood stars, because performers such as Bing Crosby and Bob Hope were golf enthusiasts. He made friends wherever he went, and in many cases, they developed into business opportunities.

He could play the game with a single-digit handicap, but he preferred the locker room, the restaurant, and talking to the press to advance his ideas. In those venues, he pursued his business ventures relating to the game.

At the luncheon, I concentrated on television. I told him that ownership would have to realize that because the puck was so small and hard to see, the absolute best camera positions needed to be secured regardless of how many seats had to be appropriated. More knowledgeable people would have to be hired in the production end. I told him that he could use all the promotional genius at his command to further interest in the game in the South and Mid-West, but people won't watch a game they don't understand. In New England, the ratings had been superb—an 18 was the average in Boston—and it was because the people had grown up with the game and understood it—they were able to fill in the details that they could not see. That 18 figure out-rated the *National Basketball Game of the Week* on NBC TV by a 3–1 margin. Some 40 years later, that analysis still applies. Hockey does not get a good national rating, which means efforts to upgrade the rights fee suffer. Amazingly, minor league hockey has sprung up all over the country. Florida supports a flock of teams because it is a great game to see in person. In Bonita Springs, Florida, a team called the Everblades packs in a 6,500 sellout crowd for every home game. Fred Corcoran tried, as a consultant, but hockey had too many hurdles to overcome, while golf simply continued to thrive with great television coverage.

Jim Hallet

The best amateur and professional golfer that Cape Cod produced in the 20th century was Jim Hallet. Some may argue that Paul Harney wins that category, but Paul is not a Cape Cod native. Hallet grew up in a golfing family, polishing his game at Bass River Golf Club and Cummaquid Golf Club. In 1982, he reached the quarterfinals of the United States Amateur championship, which was held at The Country Club in Brookline, Massachusetts. As a result, he was invited to play in the Masters the following spring. During the winter, I invited him to a Bruins game. Jim was an avid hockey fan, having been a goaltender at Dennis-Yarmouth High School, and he continued his interest at Bryant College. I interviewed him and Harry Sinden, the Bruins' general manager, and gave him a dozen Titleists with the Bruins logo prominently displayed in black and gold. The big "B" seemingly took up half the circumference of the ball.

For his first round in the Masters tournament, Hallet was paired with Arnold Palmer. To my surprise, he used the Bruins logo golf balls. Most pro golfers on the tour are well clothed in a variety of company logos, but none of them have as yet chosen to put one on a golf ball. Of course, a close-up reveals the golf ball manufacturer— Titleist, Top Flight, Precept, et al. Hallet's display of the Bruins logo at first caused consternation in the comments of the announcers. They could see it, but they didn't know what it represented.

For Hallet it proved a good luck charm. He blistered the back nine of Augusta with a 32—a record-breaking score for an amateur. He wound up with a 68, and was paired with Palmer for round number two. The Bruins got a mention finally as the name behind the logo— the announcers had done some research. Jim didn't fare so well in the rest of the tournament, but hockey fans of New England were proud of his first-round accomplishment and his inspiration to use a Bruins' logo ball. Hallet later qualified for the PGA tour, and I met with him to talk about a radio program idea. My thought was that there would be a market for a regular report from a golfer on the tour.

Each Monday, I would contact Hallet by phone and he would talk about the upcoming week—the course to be played, the likely favorites, and what part of his game he was working on. He would pass along tips and offer a variety of observations on the professional game. This would provide material for short reports on Monday, Tuesday, and Wednesday. Thursday and Friday would feature comments on his play, and Sunday would include a wrap up of his week's performance. Jim agreed to the idea. Unfortunately, I was not able to sell it, but I still think that it is a viable program.

Before his career was shortened by a hand injury, Hallet almost won for the first time in a 1991 tournament at the English Turn and Country Club in New Orleans. He finished tied for first with Ian Woosnam, but lost in the playoff. Who knows, Jim could follow in the footsteps of Allen Doyle, originally from Norwood, Massachusetts, who has gone on to great success in the Champions Tour. Allen's game blossomed when he turned 50, and he has become successful. He was a hockey star at Norwich University, and features a hockey-like swing that keeps him in contention nearly every week.

My Golf

I play a lot of golf now, but I came late to the sport. I never concentrated on the game until I was in my 50s. Once you move into the senior category in golf (generally recognized as age 55) the game becomes an important activity. With the handicap system, golf allows you to not only play, but to compete. Currently, at age 88, my handicap has drifted up to a 21, but I can—and do—compete against golfers with 8, 10, or 12 handicaps. Each year, I take a refresher course on the finer points of the game from Rick Johnson, a splendid professional who has been at Hyannisport for over 20 years.

Among the many fine programs that Rick has instituted is a senior competition every Tuesday that runs for about nine months out of the year. Players are grouped into four-man teams and usually the best two of four balls count on each hole. Full handicaps are allowed, and the team with the lowest score wins a modest jackpot. As just about the oldest senior member playing, I can testify to the complete absorption of the exercise. Another challenge for the octogenarian is to shoot one's age. In 1997, at age 78 with a handicap of 14, I accomplished the feat.

As a youngster, I never played golf or caddied, but when I was courting my wife, Barbara, in 1946 and 1947, I had to take up the game. She grew up as the oldest of nine children, on Clyde Street in Brookline, opposite The Country Club. She had four brothers, Paul, Hugh, Leo, and Richard—all of whom were caddies when they were young, and good golfers. So I played with them, once in a while, without displaying much talent. When we moved to Newton in 1956, we joined the Woodland Golf Club and Barbara took up the game in earnest. She had a natural, free-flowing swing that stood her in good stead in pressure situations. She had several of those situations as she won the Woodland Ladies' title twice. My game did not improve much. In 1964, we joined the Hyannisport Club and Barbara continued her fine play and became active in the Women's Golf Association of Massachusetts. Again, she won the club championship twice. Through the years, my handicap came down, and the best I played to was a 12. Hyannisport featured many tournaments, and one of the most popular was the Milliken Cup. I played in it every year, but without much success.

In 1993, the two-day tournament used the quota system to determine the champion. It has been rated by many as the fairest and most accurate system to determine a champion as long as handicaps are accurate. The Professional Golf Association uses it once a year, and theirs is a modified system since they are all scratch players. The usual format is to take a person's handicap (mine was at 18) and deduct that figure from 36. The result was 18, and that was my quota. I would score points by getting one for a bogey, two for a par, four for a birdie, and zero for a double bogey. If I made my quota, anything over the 18 was a plus. The player with the best plus figure was the winner.

A field of 40 teed off. I was on target the first day, and finished with a plus nine—an excellent quota figure. In second place, at plus eight, was Paul Stewart, a good friend and a National Hockey League referee who had been a caddy at Hyannisport. He was in the middle of a fine career as a hockey official after appearing in 21 games as a player for Quebec. After leaving professional hockey, he tried his hand at coaching a high school team, and doing a talk show on radio, but officiating was in his genes. His grandfather, Bill Stewart, had not only been a National League umpire, but in the winter was a referee in the National Hockey League. During the 1937–38 hockey season, he was named the coach of the Chicago Blackhawks, and in an amazing performance, led them to a Stanley Cup victory.

Since Paul Stewart and I were the leaders after the first round, we were paired the second day as the last two players to tee off. In a sense it became match play. I was 74 years old, and Paul was a strapping 38.

He easily could outdrive me, but my short game had improved. On the second hole, I sank a ten-foot putt for a birdie and four big points. I kept getting no worse than a bogie on any hole, and getting by holes 10, 11, and 12, with three successive bogies, solidified my lead over Stewart, who was struggling. I eventually finished with a second day plus eight, for a two-day total of 17. Stewart could not make his quota, and so I won the tournament handily. The player who finished second was ten points behind me and Stewart finished at negative three.

Undoubtedly, I am the oldest player to win that tournament. The youngest happened to be my nephew, Hugh Mullin, who won it while he was still in high school, at age 16. A few years later, when I was 78, I accomplished another feat that was more personal. It doesn't get your name up on any billboard in the clubhouse, but it is just as rewarding—I shot my age. I was playing a round on one of those gorgeous Cape Cod summer days with Jack Crosby, Ned Handy, and Greg LaCava—the date was June 20, 1997. Thanks to Joe Gordon, golf editor of *The Boston Herald*, and reporter John Connolly, the accomplishment with an accompanying picture was detailed in the paper on June 29.

Recapping Connolly's story, I told him how, about ten years previously, I had shot a 78, and that my handicap was 15. I pointed out that my round included at least six putts in excess of 10 feet, and that I had three birdies. I played the front nine in 41, so I was not even thinking of shooting my age. To get a 41, I had to birdie the ninth hole. "The back nine has three tough holes to start with," I told him, "I bogeyed all three, then parred the 13th, and bogeyed the 14th, so I was four over. The 15th is a par three, and I knocked it on the green. From 10 feet away, I sank the putt. As we walked to the tee on number

16—a par five—I told my partners that if I got a birdie and two pars on the final three holes, I would shoot my age. I was on the 16th in three and sank about a 12-foot putt for a birdie, so I had one major accomplishment out of the way. I encountered no trouble on 17 and 18, played them in even par, and I had reached my goal."

Barbara and I took our clubs on the road as she joined me one year in a West Coast swing, and we played among others Pebble Beach, the San Francisco Country Club, and the Olympic Club where many U.S. Opens were held. Paul Kennedy, a native of Framingham, Massachusetts, was the general manager of Olympic, and had us for dinner and golf. He was a hockey fan who rooted for the Bruins.

On other occasions we were able to take summer trips to Ireland and Scotland. In Ireland we played the best in the west—LaHinch, Ballybunion, and Tralee. In Scotland we played Dunbar, Carnoustie, and Muirfield among others. At Muirfield there was no welcome mat out. You stood outside the clubhouse with your clubs, and awaited instructions from the manager as to when you could tee off. There weren't any women's tees—they made their own arrangements, as the ball for a tee off was dropped at the caddie's discretion. About a mile from Muirfield was the Gullane Golf Club, a public course. It was just as challenging as the highly regarded Muirfield and could easily be a site for a major tournament. There were two other Gullane courses in the area, and all three welcomed women.

In the heart of the village, we saw an area where six golf holes, of varying length, had been staked out. It was called the "Children's Course," and here youngsters and an occasional adult would learn the fundamentals of the game at their own pace. There was no charge, but the condition of the six holes was not exactly top notch, although they served their purpose. I have seen only one other like it on the Cape at Otis Air National Guard Station. It features artificial greens and short holes on which youngsters can get their introduction to the game.

CHAPTER FOURTEEN

The Entrepreneur

In the early '60s FM radio was starting to come into focus. Looking toward the future, I thought ownership of a station would provide the stability and security that an on-air broadcast career could not. With a friend, Ed Sullivan, a business agent for a Boston labor union who made frequent trips to Washington and had a mutual interest in ownership, I formed a corporation—Charter Broadcasting. We first pursued existing FM stations, and found one for sale via an ad in *Broadcasting Magazine*. It was on the north shore, and price was ridiculously low—$28,000. Offering it was Anthony Athanas who owned a Swampscott restaurant, and was to develop Pier 4 in Boston into one of the world's most successful and highest grossing restaurants. We met with him several times, and discovered that while he had put up the money to get the FM station going, a promoter from Philadelphia had retained the ownership. In effect, Anthony had nothing to sell. However, the experience established a good friendship, and whenever Ed Sullivan or I visited Pier 4 (which Athanas eventually built) we received VIP treatment.

Since we both summered on the Cape, our next project was to start from scratch and build an FM station. I moved to the Cape to scour the land for a tower site. We hired a Washington law firm, Dow, Lohnes, and Albertson, to begin the application process. I established local contacts to assist in the projected programming. It took a lot of work, but ultimately it paid off. We received a license on December 22, 1965. I came up with the call letters—WCOD. The problem we were facing was that the height of the tower was not sufficient. Cape Cod is a wide area that extends for over 80 miles. We needed more than a 190-foot tower to cover it. I figured we could stall the FCC, keep the license, take our time, and watch the sale of FM sets grow. Ed Sullivan was impatient, so we parted ways, but WCOD lives on and is a successful station on Cape Cod.

Kaiser Broadcasting had a television station in the offing, and had signed up the Bruins. I was to be the sports director of Channel 56. Before moving back to Boston, I was hired by Harold Putnam to do publicity and promotion work for the Battleship *USS Massachusetts*, located in Fall River, Massachusetts. I would be employed for six months, and that would take me to the Kaiser job. Putnam was a former *Globe* reporter who had been named executive director of the Battleship. With my media connections, I was to stimulate attendance at the historic museum. I thought I did a pretty good job, and so did Harold Putnam. He moved on to be regional director of the Health, Education, and Welfare Agency; and offered me a position as public information director. I was already settled in my Kaiser-Bruins job and I loved sportscasting, so I passed up the opportunity.

One of my promotions for the *USS Massachusetts* resulted in a little contretemps with former First Lady Jacqueline Kennedy. In 1967, my good friend Dick Rougeau was a summer policeman on the staff of the Barnstable Police Department on Cape Cod while attending Boston College Law School. His assignment was to watch over the Kennedy Compound in Hyannisport. He was quite friendly with all the children who lived there. There were so many there in the summer that Mrs. Kennedy and Eunice Shriver hired a recreational director, Sandy Eiler. I suggested to Rougeau and Eiler that a good day's outing would be a visit to the Battleship *Massachusetts*. Jackie Kennedy agreed with the proposal with one stipulation—no pictures were to be taken. Rougeau, the policeman, was to accompany the group to see that law and order prevailed. As a promotion man, I could not pass up the opportunity for some much-needed publicity, and despite Mrs. Kennedy's request, I assigned a photographer. The result? A picture of Caroline Kennedy, seated on a 40-millimeter gun aiming skyward. It made papers all over the country with the site clearly indicated—the Battleship *Massachusetts,* Fall River, Massachusetts. I understood that Mrs. Kennedy was furious, and the target of her anger was Dick Rougeau. She protested to the police chief, and while Rougeau was not fired, he was reassigned to another area.

Rougeau had ambitions to be a sportscaster, and while at Boston College, initiated play-by-play of Boston College basketball on the college radio station. When Bob Cousy was named head coach of basketball at B.C., Rougeau suggested we broadcast the games at WEEI. I did some play-by-play, and Rougeau was the analyst. Since recruiting is the primary function of a successful basketball coach, Cousy had some pluses going for him. Red Auerbach spotted a talented player named Johnny Austin in the Washington area. Cousy was able to get him into B.C., and built some teams around him that were highly successful.

While Rougeau was in Boston College Law School in 1967, Channel 56 had lost the Bruins broadcast rights, so I suggested that we do some B.C. basketball games. With Dick's help we were able to do five games, and enhance the magical Cousy name with the coverage. Although I was able to call the play-by-play of a basketball game, I had no real "feel" for the game. Not many men my age who grew up in Brighton played the game. Ninety percent of the guys from my high school class played hockey in the winter. The other 10 percent who wanted to pursue basketball had to use the Brighton High School gym, which had limited availability. Rougeau later set up a successful law practice on the Cape, the firm of Rougeau, Butler, and Largay.

Birdseye Golf Classic

The veteran Joey Sindelar won the Wachovia Golf Championship in May 2004. It was his first win in 14 years. What intrigued me was the logo on his cap—Birdseye. I watch a lot of golf, but I have never seen any other player with that logo. It made me think of 1974, a time when the Bruins were riding high, and I was able to sell Bill Flynn, the general manager of TV 38, on putting a videotaped golf show on Sunday nights at 7 p.m. just before Bruins games.

I had been tossing around an idea I had for a golf competition with Tom Niblet, a friend and owner of Holly Ridge Golf Course. It was a par three located in Sandwich, Massachusetts. The idea was to have three golfers who represented one golf course, compete against three others from a different course. Each team would consist of the club professional, a female and a male. They had to be members, and hopefully, since the pro would be in charge, she/he would bring her/his club champions. The idea of having a female competitor was that the play would take place on par-three holes. Working with George Weymss, executive director of the New England PGA, we would field 16 teams. Each head-to-head competition was to be videotaped for a one-hour show, and since four of them could be done in one day, we would produce a 15-week series in four days.

Bill Flynn did not charge for the airtime, but a sponsor was needed to cover the cost of production, which entailed a crew of 18, cameras, cables, and a production truck. I suggested to Niblet that we make a pilot program to show to potential sponsors. We hired a lone cameraman to film the action, and we lined up two teams. The result was pretty primitive; but in the course of play, one of the participants almost scored a hole in one. We were making it a three-hole match using the first hole at Holly Ridge from 140 yards, the 18th hole at 150 yards, and back to the first hole for a range of 165 yards. As short as the three holes were, it was a difficult job for the cameraman to follow the play. The result was a black-and-white film with no replays.

We set up an interview with Gene Merkert, a wholesale distributor of food products in Canton, Massachusetts. He was a golfer at the Charles River Country Club, and his executive assistant, Carl Whitman, was a golfer at Pocasset Country Club on the Cape. Our presentation climaxed with the film, and both of them were excited about the "almost" hole in one. A week later they called and agreed to sponsor the series. It was to be called the *Birdseye Golf Classic*.

Whether the Birdseye company paid the bill, or Merkert thought it would help his company in their relationship with the frozen food organization, we did not know. The show went on, and when the 15-week series was completed, the Rhode Island Country Club was the winner. It was a harrowing four days. The crew was inexperienced, graphics were just about nonexistent, and delays in setting up the cameras and cables destroyed any tempo for the players. However, George Weymss was delighted and assured his operation's support in future endeavors. Gene Merkert was enthusiastic and ready to tape a second series, but the whole project was too overwhelming for the station. Bill Flynn said no.

Tucker Anthony Golf Classic

Thirteen years went by before I was able to revive the *Golf Classic* at Holly Ridge. David D'Alessandro was marketing director of John Hancock Financial Services in Boston. He was on his way up the corporate ladder at John Hancock, and was to become the CEO. He was investing a lot of money in sponsoring the Boston Marathon. Jogging and running had become a big recreation activity. I thought that the demographics of a golf television series would offer more of the type of audience that Hancock wanted. Tom Niblet and I had a friend, Ed McNamara, a former police commissioner of Boston, who knew D'Alessandro. We discussed the possibility of Hancock sponsoring the Golf Classic on NESN. The cable channel was only a couple of years old, and was growing with its coverage of Red Sox and Bruins games, but they had a lot of hours to fill. They agreed to carry the golf program at no charge if I could get it produced.

McNamara, Niblet, and I had lunch with D'Alessandro. I made a strong pitch, pointing out the growth of golf, the demographics, the association with the finest golf clubs in the area, the fact that the program would appeal to women, and on and on. I could tell almost from the start that D'Alessandro had little interest in my presentation, but he was nice enough to hear me out. At the end, he said that John Hancock would not be interested, but they had recently acquired a brokerage house in Boston—Tucker Anthony. He suggested that they might be interested.

Within days we made contact with Clive Fazioli, executive vice president of Tucker Anthony. Lunch with him proved to be a different deal. Clive was an excellent golfer, a ten handicap at Salem Country Club. To my surprise, he had played in the *Birdseye Golf Classic* 13 years before when he was a member of the Indian Ridge Club. He did not have to be sold on the idea, the participants, or any phase of the program. The cost was $45,000. It was a steep price for a 15-week series on cable TV, but Clive convinced his directors, and the *Tucker Anthony Golf Classic* was launched. The Women's Golf Association of Massachusetts cooperated fully in furnishing the best women golfers in the state, the professionals had the best male amateurs; and since the pros were playing for money, the competition was top notch. Clive Fazioli proved to be an excellent analyst. His contribution first came from the tower, and later from following the players hole by hole with a wireless microphone.

His role was to take a wireless microphone onto the course and keep pace with the players. His genial attitude overcame the basic problem of every telecast—too many delays. When Tucker Anthony gave up the brokerage business, Clive obtained Moors and Cabot as a sponsor, so the series had a 17-year run in total.

In 1994 we invited celebrities to participate. Our field included Bobby Orr, Grant Fuhr, Carlton Fisk, Ray Bourque, Jeremy Roenick, Stan Mikita, and others. Teams were formed to represent charities, and Tucker Anthony contributed $10,000 to Nauset Inc. (now CapeAbilities), a non-profit organization supporting Cape Codders with disabilities. Amanda Gustafson, Peter Mahovlich, and Claude Lemieux joined forces for the win for CapeAbilities. When the new and private Ridge Club opened in Sandwich, Massachusetts, we moved the show to its last three holes. The 16th was a dogleg right and par four, the 17th was a beautiful island green at 145 yards, and the 18th was a challenging par five with water surrounding the expansive green. Coverage of those three holes proved to be a challenge for the TV38 crew. We had moved the program from NESN and secured a larger audience on WSBK-TV.

In the course of our coverage, I thought about how the CBS TV announcers make comments as they televise the Masters. Each year, they make a big deal over "Amen Corner." My thought was that the 16th hole at the Ridge Club, just where the dogleg goes into effect, could be called the "Classic Corner." Mark Ventre, the general manager of the club, thought it was an excellent idea. Right at the turn, just about where a player should hit his drive, he placed a plaque that said: "Classic Corner—Fred Cusick, 1990." It has remained there through the years, and I occasionally hear from players who have seen it. Most of them have been able to put together the Classic reference and the Tucker Anthony show.

CHAPTER FIFTEEN

Awards and Reflection

By the 1980s, with Foster Hewitt long gone, I had become something of a Grand Old Man myself. In 1988, the League honored me with the Lester Patrick Award. The award had been created by the NHL in 1966 to honor those who had made outstanding contributions to the game in the United States. It had been given to players, coaches, general managers and owners. I was the first American broadcaster to get the Patrick Award. Bob Johnson and Keith Allen were the other recipients that year. My previous honor was being named to the Media Hall of Fame in Toronto in 1984. I was also the first American broadcaster selected for that honor. Foster Hewitt, Rene Le Cavalier, and Danny Gallivan (Rene and Danny were longtime Canadian broadcasters) were also installed. I had received only a few days notice, so I was not able to make the Hall of Fame ceremony. However, I was happy to accept the Patrick Award in person from Craig Patrick at the All-Star game in St. Louis.

How I came to win the award is a bit odd. I think I was selected because of a game I broadcast on December 8, 1987. The Bruins were playing the Philadelphia Flyers at the Spectrum. Philly had a colorful goaltender named Ron Hextall. His general manager, Bobby Clarke, said he was a better puck handler than some of the Flyers defensemen. Hextall loved to roam, secure the puck, and shoot it or pass it down the ice. In the game, the Bruins were trailing by a goal with two minutes left, and their goaltender was taken out. They stormed the Philadelphia end and Hextall moved out of the net, trapped the puck, and shot it down the ice. As always, he did it with such firmness and certainty, that Clarke's comment came to mind. On the air I said, "Hextall fires that puck so hard he'll score a goal soon." The next time the Bruins drilled it in, Hextall cradled the puck in his stick, and lofted the puck down the ice into the empty net. A few other goaltenders have done it, but none probably had a sportscaster predict it 30 seconds before it happened. The clip made the rounds of TV stations around the country, and I was identified as the forecaster. I'm sure the instant fame was a factor in someone selecting me for the Patrick honor.

I had known Lynn Patrick, Lester Patrick's son, very well; he was the coach of the Bruins when I joined the team in 1952. That meant traveling by train, sitting for hours in the lounge section of the club's Pullman, and listening to Lynn's stories. The cry of nepotism went out when Lynn joined the Rangers, coached by his father, but there were no complaints once he started to play. He was a talented and high-scoring winger. The stories he told would embrace the history of the game, since his father Lester and Uncle Frank were actually in on the beginning of hockey at the start of the 20th century. They were not only two of the best players of that pioneer era, but they were also were owners, builders, and innovators who basically fashioned the game as we know it today. Their deeds, along with a fascinating history of the game, are detailed in Eric Whitehead's book *The Patricks: Hockey's Royal Family* published by Doubleday in Canada.

I was very proud to be given the Lester Patrick Award. I received a lot of congratulatory mail, but none more appreciated than a handwritten letter from Bobby Orr: "You deserve the honor and nobody has contributed more to hockey in the United States than you. As in the game of hockey itself, class always determines who will succeed, lead, and be remembered. In your case, that is proven once again. This award places you in a very select group, and all of us associated with the sport consider this honor richly deserved. I am personally very pleased to extend to you my sincerest congratulations."

Considering the source of those comments, they meant more to me than the award itself.

Bob Ryan, *Boston Globe* sports columnist and commentator on New England Sports Network and ESPN, paid me a fine tribute. Taking a sabbatical from the *Globe*, he had worked as a sports reporter for Channel Five, Boston. "During that time," he writes in the *Globe* on November 25, 1995, "I discovered how good Fred Cusick really was, and I submit is. While editing hockey pieces, I became fascinated with the grace and rhythm of his language while describing the game he loves. You could count on finding a half-dozen plays or sequences in which he would tell the story—never overstating any case—in a spirited, yet controlled, and completely literate manner. The voice rises and falls appropriately, and a Cusick summation of furious action is invariably a textbook affair. I always looked forward to doing hockey bits, and it was because I knew Cusick could make me look good."

On November 13, 2003, I was honored by the Boston/New England Chapter of the National Television Academy as one of five recipients of their Silver Circle Award. The others were Harvey Leonard, Glenn Lacton, Paul Toomey, and Patrice Wood. I carefully prepared an acceptance speech, but it could not match the effort that the Academy put together with a taped presentation that summed up my career. There was a lot of hockey in the visual work, but they dug up some other material. It was very well done. My family and relatives were there.

In 2004, I was inducted into the Massachusetts Hockey Hall of Fame Media Category along with four others, including Jack Riley, a fellow member of Hyannisport, who was in the coaches' category. I was happy to be able to pay tribute to Bob Carpenter, who was selected in the players' category. He was the first U.S.-born player to reach the 50-goal mark in the National Hockey League. He opened the gates of the NHL for American players.

Looking back on my career, I can truthfully say that I enjoyed every minute of it. It wasn't work at all, and on the rare occasions when I attended a game and was not broadcasting it, I was unhappy and restless. I did not enjoy the experience at all. I think that playing college hockey brought a certain flavor to my play-by-play. It caused things like the subconscious rise in my voice as a play developed, and my narration became more descriptive. It was also the added focus to get the identification of the player or players who assisted on the goal.

Having the opportunity to cover Bobby Orr throughout his career was a huge bonus to me. Knowing I was broadcasting or televising to a very knowledgeable hockey audience was another plus. It is a

difficult game to televise—the puck is small and the action is fast—
on the technical side. But New Englanders who grew up playing
hockey, or who had relatives or friends who played it, were able to
absorb the intricacies of the game and fill in what they couldn't see on
the screen. When they went to a game, they brought knowledge and
enthusiasm, and the Bruins appreciated it. That's why so many of
them elected to make their permanent home in the area. It is Bruins
country.

And I am happy to say it's been my country, too.

About the author

Fred Cusick was the radio and TV announcer of the Boston Bruins for 44 years. He is the first American broadcaster named to the Hockey Hall of Fame, and is the recipient of the Lester Patrick Award for contributions to hockey in the United States.

The son of Irish immigrants, Cusick grew up in Boston and played hockey, football, and baseball in his youth. He played hockey while attending Northeastern University in Boston, and was twice winner of the school's public speaking contest.

His broadcast career began in 1941 and continued until his retirement in 2002—interrupted only by Navy service during World War II. He became the Voice of the Bruins in 1952 and called more Bruins games (both on radio and TV) than any other broadcaster. In a career that spanned seven decades, Cusick also worked with the Red Sox, Celtics, and Patriots.

Cusick also created and produced radio and TV programs. A highlight was a documentary on golf-legend Francis Ouimet, the only broadcast interview of the famous golfer in existence.

Cusick and his wife, Barbara, live on Cape Cod and have four children and three grandchildren. For more information visit: www.FredCusick.com.

Celebrate the Heroes of Boston Sports
in These Other Releases from Sports Publishing!

Game of My Life:
Boston Red Sox
by Chaz Scoggins
• 6 x 9 hardcover
• 250 pages
• photos throughout
• $24.95
• 2006 release!

Voice of the Celtics:
Johnny Most's Greatest Calls
by Mike Carey with Jamie Most
• 8.5 x 11 hardcover
• 160 pages
• color photos throughout
• $29.95
• Includes audio CD narrated by
  Tommy Heinsohn!

Tales from the
Patriots Sideline
by Michael Felger
• 5.5 x 8.25 softcover
• 192 pages
• photos throughout
• $14.95
• 2006 release!
• First time in softcover!

Boston Red Sox: 2004
World Series Champions
by The Boston Herald
• 8.5 x 11 hardcover & softcover
• 128 pages
• color photos throughout
• $19.95 (hardcover)
• $14.95 (softcover)

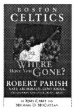

Boston Celtics:
Where Have You Gone?
by Mike Carey and
Michael D. McClellan
• 6 x 9 hardcover
• 200 pages
• photos throughout
• $19.95

Win it for...What a World
Championship Means to
Generations of Red Sox Fans
by Eric Christensen and
SonsofSamHorn.com
• 5.5 x 8.25 hardcover
• 256 pages
• photos throughout
• $24.95

Red Sox:
Where Have You Gone?
by Steve Buckley
• 6 x 9 hardcover
• 250 pages
• photos throughout
• $19.95

Boston Bruins: Greatest
Moments and Players
by Stan Fischler
• 8.5 x 11 hardcover & softcover
• 300 pages
• 100+ photos throughout
• $29.95 (hardcover)
• $19.95 (softcover)

Red Sox vs. Yankees:
The Great Rivalry
by Harvey Frommer and
Frederic Frommer
• 8.5 x 11 trade paper
• 256 pages
• photos througout
• $14.95
• Revised and Updated Edition!

Tales from the
Boston Bruins
by Kerry Keene
• 5.5 x 8.25 hardcover
• 200 pages
• photos throughout
• $19.95

All books are available in bookstores everywhere!
Order 24-hours-a-day by calling toll-free **1-877-424-BOOK (2665).**
Also order online at **www.SportsPublishingLLC.com.**

Printed in the United States
71902LV00003B/136-504